FROM CROOK TO COOK

FROM CROOK TO COOK

BY

SNOOP DOGG

WITH RYAN FORD

CHRONICLE BOOKS

SAN FRANCISCO

Martha Stewart

SNOOP AND I HAVE a special bond that dates back to when he first appeared on the *Martha Stewart Show* in 2008. Our relationship was born from our connection to food as we whipped up some cognac mashed potatoes and green brownies! It was only natural that we would reconnect by collaborating on VH1's *Martha and Snoop's Potluck Dinner Party*. Working with Snoop in the kitchen has been a remarkable learning experience for me. Not only has he taught me new lingo and cultural references, he surprised me with his unique cooking techniques and recipes. I can't wait for him to share them with the world in this fun, one of a kind cookbook!

Martha Stewart

Welcome to My Kitchen

Man, I must've been around the world and back hundreds of times during the course of damn near three decades. I spend more than half of my life on the road. And while it's hard being away from the Cali weather and of course, the green that my home turf offers, I've grown quite fond of getting up and getting out to mingle with the many fans I'm lucky enough to have earned around the globe.

From Moscow to Munich, Mississippi to Morocco, and Japan to the Motherland, it's always so surprising to see fans across the world inspired by that West Coast way we living. Like for real, they be knowing our swag, our slang, and our whole get down—and sometimes they don't even be knowing the language.

But the food on the road? Well, that's hit or miss at best. Combine that with Tha Dogg not being the most adventurous, Anthony Bourdain-type when it comes to grub, doesn't always make for the most splendid of occasions, ya dig? That's why when I hit certain cities, I know to hit certain spots where they got the right heat and flavors.

I'm far from a young pup. And like a real seasoned playa, my tastes have evolved over the years. But while I've learned how to get down with that top-notch luxury cuisine, I'm still prone to keep it way hood with some of those LBC classics.

One thing for sure and two things for certain, a Dogg's gotta eat and one way or another, we make it happen. Whether that's getting creative with some backstage vittles or remaking and remixing that one recipe I picked up on the road when I'm back at the crib in Killa Cali.

That's why it's really a no brainer to throw together some of the best from my kitchen and share it with you.

From breakfast goodies to late night munchies, there's just enough out of my stash to make sure that you're covered no matter the occasion.

We got all that good good here ready to burn—weighed and bagged for your own kitchen. What's always up in my fridge and pantry, a few Jamaican-inspired editions from my time in the islands, a couple of Down South soul staples, and some inside never-before-shared recipes from the Broadus fam to you. And it ain't just about the grub. You can't have the bites without the beats, so I got the playlists ready to rock for you and yours while you get ta whipping on that stove top.

Trust your big homie. This is the best cookbook ever made. And now it's in your hands. So put one in the air right quick...contemplate the possibilities and then figure out whatcha gonna make first!

In My Pantry

5.
SOY SAUCE

9.
INSTANT
MACARONI AND
CHEESE

10.
POP TARTS

8. KETCHUP

6. HONEY

7. TUNA

3. HOT SAUCE

2. SEASONING SALT

1. LEMON PEPPER

4. MAPLE SYRUP

In My Pantry

1
LEMON PEPPER

I can't handle no bland chicken, so I like to throw a little lemon pepper on my wings. Shout out to my man Rick Ross—he knows what's up with that lemon pepper! You can't go wrong with that McCormick brand.

2
SEASONING SALT

Let me sprinkle you with a little game right quick. Seasoning salt is a blend of paprika, turmeric, onion, and garlic, a classic you can add to anything. In the Boss Dogg's kitchen, the pantry wouldn't be complete without it! Splurge a little and get you some of that Lawry's.

3
HOT SAUCE

I'm down with all kind of sauces as you can see, but hot sauce has gotta be the most essential. Now everybody's got their favorite brand, but Tha Dogg's got a thing for Crystal. That's Louisiana's finest right there! A splash of that goes with anything—you can put it in a sandwich, on some chicken, on top of a pizza. Whatever you add it to, it's gonna kick it up a notch.

4
MAPLE SYRUP

It wouldn't be the breakfast of champions without maple syrup. Whether you got some pork on your fork or a stack of pancakes, nothing tops it all off like a stick of butter and some warm maple syrup. Let that Aunt Jemima soak in and then prepare to get your chow on.

5

SOY SAUCE

Traveling the world put me on to a lot of fine Asian cuisines—noodles, rices, sushi, and a whole lot more. Nothing goes better with that egg fried rice or sashimi than some soy sauce. You can go ahead and mix it with some of that wasabi, too—just keep that ratio right or your sinuses will be acting crazy!

6

HONEY

Ain't nuthin' more important to the Top Dogg than his vocal chords, and as a live performer, I gotta keep those in tip-top shape. A couple veterans in the game taught me the key to keeping your vocals right is some fresh honey and warm tea. I've kept the honey on deck ever since. I like that raw and unfiltered honey, 'cause I'm raw and unfiltered my damn self!

7

TUNA

Whether you're mixing it up with some mayo or grilling it in a bomb tuna melt, a can of this stuff will never steer you wrong. I'm also trying to keep my diet right, especially now that I'm going hard in the yard with my gym regimen. Fish is meant to be real good for you, so I get mines from some tuna!

8

KETCHUP

I love to get down on the grill, and what barbeque is complete without ketchup? Picture that—burgers, hot dogs, sausages—and no ketchup to smother on top? Just some meat in a dry-ass bun? Nah, not in the Dogg's household. Keep the ketchup close, and make sure it's Heinz. Yeah, don't cheat yourself; treat yourself.

9

INSTANT MACARONI AND CHEESE

Homemade mac and cheese is always gonna be the ultimate, but sometimes you need the quick fix. If you ain't prepared to wait for that made-from-scratch mac to simmer and bake, reach for that Kraft and pull out a pot. Boom, you got some cheesy goodness in a matter of minutes.

10

POP TARTS

I say they're for the kids or my grandson when he stops by, but I enjoy one of these toasted treats once in a while. They got every flavor under the sun these days, but I say keep it original and get chocolate fudge. Sometimes you gotta stick with the classics, ya dig?

In My Fridge

10.
BUTTER

2.
CHEDDAR
CHEESE

8.
MOËT

9.
ORANGE
JUICE

5.
DILL
PICKLES

6.
BARBECUE
SAUCE

1.
EGGS

7.
MUSTARD

4.
RANCH
DRESSING

3.
MILK

In My Fridge

1

EGGS

Eggs are good any way—scrambled with some cheese, fried in a sandwich, or in one of my chronic omelets. If you got a saltshaker handy, you can even boil that thang. Now that will leave you highly satisfied.

2

CHEDDAR CHEESE

I done came a long way from eating that government-issued cheese, but I remember it well! I'll still mess around and throw some Cheddar in a lot of my cooking; you'll find my Squad Up Chili Cheese Fries (page 166) and Booted and Looted Nachos (page 168) come fully loaded with the stuff. One way or another, Bigg Snoop Dogg is all about getting that cheese!

3

MILK

Remember in *Friday* when my man Cube ran out of milk and had to put water on his cereal? That's never happening in my household. I keep the milk on deck since I'm always ready for a big bowl of Snoop's Loops. Miss me with that almond or soy milk. I like mine's ice cold—skim or 2% is just fine.

4

RANCH DRESSING

Another condiment of choice. I'm starting to adapt to eating vegetables and salads and all that, but I'm gonna need some ranch to give all those greens some extra flavor. That creamy dressing is exactly what I need to make all that plant food a little more tasteful. As far as what kind, Hidden Valley is the way to go. Their ranch is real cool and smooth—a li'l something like yours truly.

5

DILL PICKLES

What comes with every deli sandwich you've ever seen? That pickle, Jack! Whether it's pastrami piled high or classic roast beef, you know you gotta have that pickle on the side. The same is true when I make one of my Caribbean Queen Cubanos (page 58) at home. I like to throw that pickle on there to complete the whole thang.

6

BARBECUE SAUCE

As I said, I like to helm the grill once in a while and get my Iron Chef on. Another essential component of any barbecue is this sauce. Whether you're marinating your meat in it or just throwing a dollop on top, barbecue sauce gives you that sweet, tangy taste I can't get enough of. The best sauce out there, you ask? Well, you're gonna have to holler at my Uncle Reo about that. Please believe Reo's Ribs held it down with the finest sauce in the land.

7

MUSTARD

Nah, I'm not talking about my producer partna "Mustard on the Beat," I'm talking about that Heinz mustard, that French's mustard, that mellow yellow. It's another condiment you gotta have, you understand me? Mustard also sets my OG Fried Bologna (page 50) off just right. It ain't complete without it!

8

MOËT

Sometimes you just gotta embrace that rap star lifestyle. I like to enjoy a glass of bubbly now and then, and when I do, I gotta have the best. That's why I keep a bottle of Moët chilled—I stay ready to get it poppin'.

9

ORANGE JUICE

I'ma kinda on my li'l health kick right now and drawn more to the green variety. But hey, you know there ain't nuthin' like OJ. You have to keep a jug of this at play at all times. You never know when you might need to mix it with some Moët or better yet... gin. Yeah you saw that one coming right?

10

BUTTER

The key to all good cooking—butter, and lots of it. And I'm not talkin' about that low-fat vegetable spread. I'm talking about that real deal Holyfield that's churned and yellow and ready to sizzle on the pan. A stick or two is always gonna be found at Snoop's spot.

TOP
of the
SPOTS

These are my main get downs to get my grub on. Of course, most of these fall into my backyard—the CITY OF ANGELS. No need for Yelping when you come to MY city. But the Dogg does get out...and me and the BIG APPLE go way back. So I got one of those in the chamber for you as well.

~ 1 ~
ROSCOE'S

Shit, ever since I've been in Hollywood I've been going to Roscoe's. I was first introduced to it when I was working with Dr. Dre on *The Chronic*. And Roscoe's has always been good to me. Man, people never thought chicken and waffles could work, but they broke the code. Their food is so good and we love the way they expanded. Now everyone around the world is fiendin' for chicken and waffles. Well, I've tried this pairing all over and I'ma let you know—you gotta come to one of the Roscoe's locations in L.A. to get that real deal Holyfield. That buttery waffle and those succulent wings are so good, my man President Obama had to get him some! Now three wings and a waffle is known as the Obama Special. Can you dig that?

~ 2 ~
RANDY'S DONUTS

Inglewood! Always up to no good. When you see that giant donut, you know you all in the I. This iconic place is just a few blocks away from my L.A. compound so I'm always down to run and go grab a couple boxes and get the homies right before a Madden tourney. Randy's don't try too hard to give you all those fancy pastries; they give you the flavors you love and they do it right. So grab a maple bar, a chocolate ring, or both if it's a cheat day. Whatever you pick up at Randy's, you're gonna leave sweetly satisfied.

~ 3 ~
FATBURGER

The late, great Biggie said it best...If you wanna flirt her, take her to Fatburger. An L.A. staple long before In-N-Out was all the rage. Whenever all the rappers used to come to L.A. for The Source Awards, you knew where to find them...the Fatburger by the Beverly Center. But they just might get jacked if they didn't check in. It's still the City of Angels and constant danger.

~ 4 ~
THE SERVING SPOON

This little-known food spot is really a ghetto superstar and has the best breakfast in the city! Salmon croquettes, chicken wings, grits, and, of course, those cheesy eggs. But don't even think about trying to slide in Sunday morning after church. That thang is all of the way packed like the club be on Saturday night. But it's worth it.

~ 5 ~
THE W HOTEL
NEW YORK CITY

New York, New York, big city of dreams. Yeah, if you know my history then you know that the East Coast has love for Snoop Dogg. Out of any place outside of Killa Cali, I've hit the city that never sleeps the most over the last three decades. I know it well.
Since a Dogg's gonna roam, The W Hotel, smack dab in the middle of the Big Apple, is like my second home. I pretty much stay room serviced up really, but I feel like I'm set up like a real boss in the back of the dining room. I've got my go-to order and they always know what it is right when Tha Dogg walks through the door. Now that's service.

CHAPTER 1

Break-fast

Tha Smoovie [23]

Not Ya Mamma's Corn Muffins [24] Stack'd Up Flap Jacks [26] Cinnamon Rollin' [27] Biscuits with Tha Thickness Gravy [30] OG Breakfast [34] Ashford and Simpson Eggs [35] Billionaire's Bacon [36] Mile-High Omelet [39]

MORNING, SCRUBS! Time to wake yourself up, and what better way than with the most important meal of the day? When it comes to kicking the day off, I've always been a cereal guy. I've been known to keep a box of Lucky Charms or Cheerios close, and I even mentioned them in a couple of my rhymes back in the day. Don't get it twisted though, 'cause I can do a lot more than dust off a box of Frosted Flakes. I've been whippin' up some eggs since I was a youngster—in fact, I used to work the breakfast shift at McDonald's as a kid. The supervisor would call me Young Eggs 'cause I could crack the eggshell with one hand—you better ask somebody! I still be putting that skill to good use when I'm cheffin' in the kitchen, putting together a hearty breakfast for my grandson. This chapter has a few Dogg-approved recipes to kickstart your day, so rise and shine and let's get cookin'...

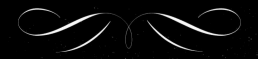

Tha Smoovie

You've probably noticed I've been going bodyguard-hard in the gym. Yeah, I've been hitting the weights, running drills, and taking care of the mind, body, and spirit. I also gotta make sure I finish a workout with my favorite smoothie—I don't just be smokin' green, I drink my greens, too!

SERVES 1

INGREDIENTS

2   cups [40 g] fresh spinach
1   medium orange, peeled and quartered
1   medium banana, sliced
2   cups [480 ml] coconut water
2   Tbsp protein powder (optional)

In a blender, combine the spinach, orange, banana, coconut water, and protein powder (if using). Blend on high speed until smooth and creamy. Serve immediately.

THA FLIP

Mix it up with pineapple, apples, kale, or whatever you got on deck. The point is to get the fuel to get you through your day.

Not Ya Mamma's Corn Muffins

I got a lot of love for the corn bread at Roscoe's, especially with a little butter and some jelly. I even took my man Larry King to the Hollywood location one time, and had to put him up on how good that corn bread is. Don't get it confused though—my homemade corn bread muffins are nothing to play with! I put 'em up against anyone's, so go ahead and taste for yourself. What makes 'em so good? Maybe it's that sour cream in the mix. I know what you're thinking—"Corn bread and sour cream?" Don't knock it 'til you've tried it.

SERVES 6 TO 8
MAKES 12 MUFFINS

INGREDIENTS
1   cup [140 g] all-purpose flour
⅔   cup [90 g] yellow cornmeal
1½ tsp baking powder
½   tsp salt
¼   tsp baking soda
4   Tbsp [55 g] unsalted butter, at room temperature
¼   cup [50 g] granulated sugar
2   large eggs
½   cup [120 ml] whole milk
⅔   cup [160 g] sour cream, or full-fat plain yogurt

1. Preheat the oven to 425°F [220°C], with a rack in the middle position. Butter or insert liners into a 12-cup muffin tin and set aside.

2. In a small bowl, whisk the flour, cornmeal, baking powder, salt, and baking soda to combine.

3. In a medium bowl, combine the butter and sugar. Using a handheld electric mixer or a stand mixer with the paddle attachment, beat on medium speed until creamy. Add the eggs and beat until golden and blended. Stir in the milk and sour cream.

4. Gradually add the dry ingredients to the wet. Gently mix or beat at low speed until just combined, being careful not to over-mix (the batter should be very thick).

5. Spoon the batter into the prepared muffin cups, filling each about three-fourths full.

6. Place the muffin tin in the oven and bake for 16 to 18 minutes, rotating the muffin tin halfway through the baking time to ensure even cooking. The muffins are done when they are golden brown and a toothpick inserted into the center of the muffins comes out clean.

7. Remove the muffin tin from the oven and place it on a wire rack. Let the muffins rest for 5 minutes, or until cool enough to touch. Remove from the pan and serve warm.

8. Store the muffins at room temperature, in an airtight container or ziplock bag, for up to 3 days, or in the freezer for up to 2 months.

Stack'd Up Flap Jacks

I like my pancakes just like I like my money—stacked high to the ceiling. This pancake recipe is always worth whippin' up. Just make sure you got plenty of butter and Aunt Jemima on deck because nothing takes these pancakes to the next level like a drizzle of that sticky, sweet syrup. Ya dig?

SERVES 4 TO 6

INGREDIENTS

2½ cups [300 g] cake flour or all-purpose flour
¾ tsp salt
2½ Tbsp granulated sugar
2½ Tbsp baking powder
2 large eggs
2 tsp pure vanilla extract
1¾ cups [420 ml] whole milk
5 Tbsp [75 g] sour cream
6 Tbsp [90 g] unsalted butter, melted, and cooled slightly, plus 1 Tbsp butter for the pan and more for serving
Maple syrup, for serving

1. In a medium bowl, whisk the flour, salt, sugar, and baking powder. Set aside.

2. In a large bowl, whisk the eggs, vanilla, milk, and sour cream until frothy. Add the melted butter and whisk again.

3. Using a sieve, sift the dry ingredients over the wet and gently fold with a rubber spatula to combine. Do not overmix; stop when the batter is still a bit lumpy and thin.

4. Place a large skillet over medium- to medium-high heat and add 1 Tbsp of butter. Swirl the pan to cover the bottom completely. Once the skillet is hot and the foam has subsided, pour ¼-cup [60-ml] portions of batter into the pan. Cook until the bubbles in the center of the pancakes burst, and when you lift an edge with your spatula it looks lightly brown. Carefully flip and cook the other side until golden.

5. Serve immediately with butter and some Aunt Jemima.

THA FLIP

Go straight bananas by putting 3 or 4 thin slices of that fruit right on the pancake before it starts bubbling.

Cinnamon Rollin'

I'm always down for a treat with a little cinnamon in it to mix things up. Cinnamon Toast Crunch is cool when I'm in my cereal mode, but there's no better cinnamon snack than these rolls. I'm telling you—these things are sweet and spice and everything nice. Get you one—matter fact, get two! And don't trip on that bourbon; it ain't gonna get you pulled over. It's just enough to give it that special twang.

SERVES 6 TO 8
MAKES 12 CINNAMON ROLLS

FOR THE DOUGH:

¼ cup [60 ml] whole milk
2¼ tsp instant yeast
2 Tbsp granulated sugar
1 large egg
2 Tbsp unsalted butter, at room temperature
2½ cups [350 g] all-purpose flour
1 tsp salt
3 Tbsp unsalted butter, melted

FOR THE CINNAMON FILLING:

⅔ cup [130 g] packed brown sugar
1 tsp ground cinnamon

FOR THE BOURBON GLAZE:

1 cup [120 g] confectioners' sugar, plus more as needed
2 Tbsp heavy cream, plus more as needed
2 Tbsp bourbon

TO MAKE THE DOUGH:

1. Oil a large bowl and set aside.

2. In a small saucepan over medium heat, combine ½ cup [120 ml] of water and the milk. Heat for 2 to 3 minutes until warm. Transfer the warmed liquid to a large bowl and sprinkle on the yeast to activate (it should start foaming).

3. Add the sugar, egg, and softened butter. Stir until well combined and smooth.

4. Gradually add the flour and salt. Stir to combine until a wet dough begins to form. Transfer the dough to the bowl of a stand mixer with the dough hook attachment. Beat at medium speed for 6 to 7 minutes. Alternatively, transfer the dough to a floured surface and knead for 8 minutes until a sticky ball begins to form. Transfer the kneaded dough to the prepared bowl and cover with plastic wrap or a warm cloth. Let sit for 1 to 1½ hours until the dough doubles in size.

CONTINUED

TO MAKE THE CINNAMON FILLING:

In a small bowl, stir together the brown sugar and cinnamon until well blended. Set aside.

TO MAKE THE BOURBON GLAZE:

In a small bowl, stir together the confectioners' sugar, cream, and bourbon until smooth, adding more cream or sugar, as needed, so the mixture is easily drizzled. Set aside.

TO MAKE THE CINNAMON ROLLS:

1. Preheat the oven to 350°F [180°C], with a rack in the middle position. Butter a 9-by-13-in [23-by-33-cm] baking dish and set aside.

2. Place the dough on a lightly floured surface and roll it into a 6-by-18-in [15-by-46-cm] rectangle. Brush the dough with the melted butter.

3. Sprinkle the cinnamon filling evenly over the dough. Starting at the 18-in [46-cm] edge, tightly roll the dough into a log. When you reach the end, moisten the edge with water before sealing the roll. Cut the roll crosswise into 12 slices and arrange them in the prepared baking dish, cut-side down.

4. Place the dish in the oven and bake for 25 minutes, rotating the dish halfway through the baking time to ensure even cooking. The cinnamon rolls are done when they are golden brown.

5. Remove the rolls from the oven and drizzle the glaze over the warm rolls. Serve immediately.

6. The cinnamon rolls will keep at room temperature in an airtight container or ziplock bag for 3 days, or in the freezer for up to 2 months.

BISCUITS

with

THA THICKNESS GRAVY

SERVES
6 TO 8
MAKES
10 BISCUITS

If you've been **DOWN SOUTH** then you ate this on plenty of day-breaks. This is that real soul food classic. The key here is to get those biscuits **FLUFFY**. And that gravy, well that's gotta be like that humid air of a **DIRTY SOUTH** summer—extra, super thick. But eat too much of this and you might as well just take your ass right back to bed. This ain't for **THE MEEK**. It'll put your ass right back to sleep.

FOR

THA BISCUITS

- 2 cups [280 g] all-purpose flour, plus more for the work surface
- 1 cup [120 g] cake flour
- 1½ Tbsp granulated sugar
- 1 Tbsp baking powder
- ¾ tsp salt
- 2¼ cups [540 ml] heavy cream
- 1 large egg
- ¼ tsp salt

FOR

THA THICK-NESS GRAVY

- 1 lb [455 g] breakfast sausage
- ¼ cup [35 g] all-purpose flour
- 1 cup [240 ml] whole milk
- 1 cup [240 ml] heavy cream
- Cracked black pepper

THA BISCUITS

1. Line a baking sheet with parchment paper and set aside.

2. In a large bowl, whisk the all-purpose flour, cake flour, sugar, baking powder, and salt to combine. Add the cream. Using a wooden spoon, or your hands, combine the wet ingredients into the dry until a shaggy dough forms.

3. Transfer the dough to a lightly floured work surface and knead it a few times until it is smooth and no longer shaggy, re-flouring your work surface, if necessary. Gently pat the dough into a rectangle about 1 in [2.5 cm] thick. Using a 3-in [7.5-cm] biscuit cutter dipped in flour, cut out biscuits from the dough rectangle and place them on the prepared sheet. Collect the scraps, re-pat, and cut, as needed.

4. Place the biscuits, on the baking sheet, into the freezer and freeze for 1 hour.

5. Preheat the oven to 425°F [220°C], with a rack in the top third of the oven.

6. In a small bowl, whisk the egg and salt until well blended. Remove the biscuits from the freezer and brush the tops of the frozen biscuits with the egg wash.

7. Place the biscuits in the oven and bake for 5 minutes. Decrease the temperature to 400°F [200°C] and bake for about 13 minutes more, rotating the pan halfway through the baking time to ensure even cooking. The biscuits are ready when they are golden brown on top and lightly browned on the bottom. Remove the biscuits from the oven and let them sit for 1 to 2 minutes on the baking sheet until they are easy to handle.

8. To serve, break the biscuits apart with your hands, spread with butter, and top with sausage gravy.

9. The biscuits will keep at room temperature in an airtight container or ziplock bag for 3 days, or in the freezer for up to 2 months.

THA THICKNESS GRAVY

1

Heat a large skillet over medium heat. Crumble the sausage into the skillet. Cook for about 10 minutes until the meat is no longer pink, using a wooden spoon to break it up and stir occasionally.

2

Sprinkle the sausage with the flour. Cook until the flour absorbs the fat, about 1 minute. Slowly dribble in the milk and cream, stirring constantly. Raise the heat to medium-high and simmer for 5 to 10 minutes until thickened, stirring constantly.

3

Season with pepper (salt isn't necessary; the sausage should be salty enough) and serve immediately with the biscuits.

4

The gravy will keep tightly covered in the refrigerator for up to 3 days. Gently rewarm on the stovetop over medium heat, or in the microwave.

OG Breakfast:

WAKEY, WAKEY, EGGS AND BACY

My kids are grown and up outta the crib now. But when they were younger, I used to love it when my wife would hit them with that classic breakfast: eggs, bacon, and toast. You can bet that I'ma sneak in right beside them, PJs on and everything, and make sure I get a plate of that as well. Good morning sunshine!

We ain't talking Denny's or IHOP here. We talking your mom, my mom, shit, everyone's mom knows how to whip up this one real quick. And if you ain't telling time with a sundial, you can always get this one cracking for the squad after one of them late night sessions, ya dig?

Crispy Bacon

Make sure you fry that bacon hard. We stay crispy on this side.

SERVES 4

INGREDIENTS
8   slices thick-cut bacon

1. Lay 4 bacon slices in a single layer in a large skillet. Line a plate with paper towels and set aside.

2. Turn the heat under the skillet to medium. Cook for 4 to 5 minutes until brown and crispy. Flip and cook the other side for 4 to 5 minutes until crispy. Transfer to the prepared plate and repeat with the remaining bacon slices.

3. Discard or save the grease in an airtight jar for later use.

4. Serve with Ashford and Simpson Eggs (opposite) and toast.

Ashford and Simpson Eggs

Honestly, I don't even understand why you'd wanna eat eggs without cheese. The perfect food duo. Good for first thing when you open your eyes when that cock-a-doodle doos, or right before you shut it down and the sandman takes over. The two go together like peanut butter and jelly, like Magic and Kareem, like Cheech and Chong.

SERVES 4

INGREDIENTS

8   large eggs
6   Tbsp [90 ml] whole milk
    Salt
    Cracked black pepper
2   Tbsp unsalted butter
1   cup [80 g] shredded
    Cheddar cheese

1. In a medium bowl, combine the eggs and milk. Season with salt and pepper. Using a fork, beat well to combine.

2. In a large skillet over medium-high heat, melt the butter. Swirl the skillet to cover the bottom completely.

3. Once the skillet is hot and the foam has subsided, pour in the eggs. While the eggs cook, using a heat-proof spatula, slowly drag the edges of the egg toward the center, making large waves in the pan until the curds are almost set, 2 to 3 minutes.

4. Remove the pan from the heat and sprinkle on the cheese. The cheese should melt after a minute or so. Taste and season with more salt and pepper, as needed. Serve immediately with Crispy Bacon (opposite) and toast.

Billionaire's Bacon

This is for when you on some real player shit and ain't got time for that regular swine. I've heard this called Millionaire's Bacon—some black pepper for that smoke, a little fire from some red pepper flakes, and a heap of brown sugar like D'Angelo, and you've just fried up a pile of Uncle Snoopy's *Billionaire* Bacon. Like my guy Justin Timberlake, as my other homie Sean Parker, said in that Zuckerberg flick *The Social Network*, "A million dollars isn't cool. You know what's cool? A billion dollars." Now eat up and go get that!

SERVES 4

INGREDIENTS

½   cup [100 g] packed light brown sugar
1   tsp cracked black pepper
1   tsp red pepper flakes
8   slices thick-cut bacon

1. Preheat the oven to 400°F [200°C], with a rack in the top third of the oven. Line a baking sheet with aluminum foil, place a wire rack on top of the foil, and set aside.

2. In a small bowl, stir together the brown sugar, black pepper, and red pepper flakes.

3. Lay the bacon slices on the rack. Spread the brown sugar mixture evenly over the bacon.

4. Place the baking sheet in the oven and bake for 25 to 30 minutes, rotating the baking sheet halfway through the baking time to ensure even cooking. The bacon is done when it's crispy and glazed.

5. Remove the baking sheet from the oven and cool the bacon for 5 minutes on the rack. Serve warm with Ashford and Simpson Eggs (page 35) or in the Mile-High Omelet (page 39).

Mile-High Omelet

So now you sittin' on some stacks with that Billionaire's Bacon and thinking, *What could possibly come next?* Yes, a wise man named Meek once said there were levels to this shit...even breakfast. So let's take it up a notch, why don't we? Keep the fire on that pan, chop some onions, break that bacon into bits, crack some eggs, and baby we can whip it. Whip it right. Right into the pan that is. Now grab Mrs. Butterworth and douse that omelet with more flavor than a Life Saver. This a big-timer's breakfast feast. So don't cheat yourself; treat yourself.

SERVES 2

INGREDIENTS

4   large eggs
½   tsp salt
½   tsp cracked black pepper, plus more for seasoning
2   Tbsp unsalted butter
½   cup [40 g] shredded sharp Cheddar cheese
1   Tbsp chopped fresh chives, plus more for garnishing
4   Billionaire's Bacon slices (page 36), 2 whole, 2 chopped

1. In a small bowl, whisk the eggs, 2 Tbsp of water, the salt, and pepper until the whites and yolks are well combined and the mixture is frothy. Set aside.

2. In a large nonstick skillet over medium-high heat, melt the butter. Swirl the skillet to coat the bottom.

3. When the skillet is hot and the foam has subsided, pour the egg mixture into the center and tilt the skillet in all directions to cover the bottom.

4. As the eggs start to set, using a heat-proof spatula, gently lift the edges of the omelet toward the middle, letting the uncooked egg flow beneath the omelet and toward the edges of the skillet. The eggs are done when the bottom is set and the edges look crisp (the top will still look wet), 3 to 4 minutes.

5. Sprinkle the Cheddar and chives down the middle of the omelet. Cook for 30 seconds more. Place 2 slices of bacon on top of the Cheddar and chives.

6. With your spatula, fold the omelet in half. Tilt the skillet to slide the omelet toward the edge, carefully transferring it to a serving plate.

7. Season with pepper and garnish with chives and the chopped bacon. Serve warm.

OG MUNCHIES

*

CEREAL ROUNDUP

~ 1 ~

LUCKY CHARMS

This ain't talkin' about those colorful diamonds in your new Johnny Dang–designed grill. This that little leprechaun, and he seems to be really on to something. Ain't nothing like getting a whole spoonful of marshmallows. Can you believe it? Oh, wow. That's when you know that good ol' Lady Luck has got your back.

HONEY NUT CHEERIOS

Now there's Cheerios in the yellow box, but we on a higher level. When a bowl of those dry-ass Os won't do the trick, get down with the brown. I'm talking about those Cheerios in the brown box. That li'l bee stung those Os with that sweetness that makes your taste buds pop—when you get that special craving. Know what I mean?

3

WHEATIES

The breakfast of champions! Now they know they should've had the Big Boss Dogg on that damn box years ago. That's all right though, cuz before I get out on the court for one of those celeb games, you know I grab me a bowlful. Next up? Snoop Dogg presents Weedies. Now that's got a ring to it.

FRUIT LOOPS

All those colors drew me in when I was a kid on my Toucan Sam shit. But, damn, don't all the colors taste the exact same? The best part about eating this is slurping up that rainbow-colored milk right after. Big Snoopy's still a kid at heart—aren't we all? *Snoop Loops* anyone?

PEANUT BUTTER CAP'N CRUNCH

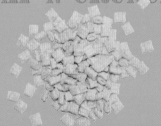

I don't know if these actually taste like peanut butter or Cap'n Crunch, but that savory sweetness mixed with a little of that "you hear me" and next thing you know, you're waking up with a bunch of crumbs in your lap. WARNING: Eating too many of these bad boys will have the top of your mouth feeling rawer than a carpet burn. Listen to Tha Dogg!

CHAPTER 2

Lunch

Chop it Up! Salad [45]

The King Classic

Caesar [46]   The Lunch

Briz-eak [48]   Get That

Bread Sub [49]   OG Fried

Bologna Sandwich [50]

Mississippi Catfish

Sandwich [54]   Caribbean

Queen Cubano [58]

No-Limit Po' Boy [60]

SOME OF MY most memorable lunches took place at my old high school, Long Beach Poly High. Man, me and the homies used to have a blast during those lunch periods. We would be hanging out in the canteen, and I would buss my freestyle raps while one of my boys banged on the tables to create a beat. Those are some of my earliest memories of really getting down as a rapper. When we weren't rapping, we would bag on each other—joke about what the homies were wearing, what they looked like, whatever was around at the time. The only bad memories about those school lunches? The actual food. Man, those cafeteria meals were nasty back then! Well, you can best believe my lunch options have improved since I was a student ditching classes. Peep this next section to see the kind of mid-day meals I be enjoying nowadays...

Chop it Up! Salad

A boss midday delight. When I think of famous gangstas, I think of none other than Vito Corleone, yeah The *GAWDFATHER*. But we all know that Vito was a little too gordo. But me...The Doggfather? They don't call me Slim with the tilted brim just because. But best believe you can keep it gangsta at a meeting with the bosses without slurping up a plate of pasta. Keep that shit all the way G and pull out a salad on they asses. But let 'em know, ain't nothing sweet on this side of the table. We got that salami and you already know that we gettin' that provolone, too. So grab the sharpest knife you got and get ta choppin', *capeesh*?

SERVES 2

FOR THE VINAIGRETTE:
½ cup [120 ml] balsamic vinegar
1 cup [240 ml] extra-virgin olive oil
1 Tbsp whole-grain or Dijon mustard
1 tsp dried oregano
   Salt
   Cracked black pepper

FOR THE SALAD:
½ head romaine lettuce, chopped
½ cucumber, chopped
½ medium tomato, chopped
1 15-oz [430-g] can chickpeas, drained and rinsed
½ cup [160 g] Kalamata olives, pitted and chopped
1 cup Provolone cheese [320 g] cut into ½-in [12-mm] cubes
1 cup salami [340 g] cut into ½-in [12-mm] cubes

TO MAKE THE VINAIGRETTE:
In a small bowl or jar with a lid, combine the vinegar, olive oil, mustard, and oregano. Season with salt and pepper. Whisk, or cover the jar and shake vigorously, until combined. Taste and add more salt and pepper, as needed. Set aside.

TO MAKE THE SALAD:
1. In a large bowl, combine the lettuce, cucumber, tomato, chickpeas, olives, cheese, and salami.

2. Add the vinaigrette (shaking or whisking again, if needed) and toss the salad until well coated in the dressing. Serve immediately.

The King Classic Caesar

Nothing like a classic Caesar for lunch.

SERVES 2

FOR THE DRESSING:

2 garlic cloves, chopped
2 Tbsp freshly squeezed lemon juice
1 Tbsp Dijon mustard
2 tsp Worcestershire sauce
1 cup [240 g] mayonnaise
⅓ cup [80 ml] olive oil
½ cup [15 g] grated Parmesan cheese
1 tsp anchovy paste
½ tsp cracked black pepper

FOR THE SALAD:

2 boneless skinless chicken breasts
½ tsp salt
½ tsp cracked black pepper
2 heads romaine lettuce
½ cup [40 g] croutons
½ cup [15 g] grated Parmesan cheese
1 Tbsp chopped chives
1 lemon, cut into wedges

TO MAKE THE DRESSING:
In a medium bowl, whisk the garlic, lemon juice, mustard, and Worcestershire sauce until smooth. Whisk in the mayonnaise, olive oil, Parmesan cheese, anchovy paste, and pepper. Set aside.

TO MAKE THE SALAD:

1. Place a grill pan over medium-high heat.

2. Sprinkle the chicken breasts evenly with the salt and pepper. Place the chicken in the pan. Grill for 4 to 5 minutes per side, or until the internal temperature reaches 165°F [75°C] when measured with an instant-read thermometer. Let cool completely. Slice each breast into 6 pieces.

3. Arrange the romaine lettuce leaves on a platter. Top with the croutons and sliced chicken. Sprinkle with the Parmesan cheese and chives. Drizzle with the dressing, serving any extra on the side with the lemon wedges. Serve immediately.

THA FLIP

How does Bigg Snoop put a spin on the classic Caesar? Swap that chicken breast for Get Tha Chip Fried Chicken Wings (page 80), and plenty of 'em, too. That piece of meat is a little bit easier to chew. It's smoother. So I flip it and strip it. Yank that meat off the bone and sprankle, yes I said S-P-R-A-N-K-L-E, some of that good ol' wing meat on there. Yeah...just like that.

The Lunch Briz-eak

C'mon dog...it's just us. You ain't gotta lie to kick it. You know you really ain't rushing out to get food on your lunch break. You just dippin' out for a quick smoke sesh cuz. We already know. That's cool, do you. I ain't trippin'. But on those days when you really gotta get some work done and ain't got even a minute to grab a sammich—grab some apples, some grapes, a little of this and a little of that, mixed with some honey and peanut butter...now you got the energy to deal with your punk-ass coworkers for the rest of the day. And hey, yo—spray a little something on yourself before you dip back in, you wanna keep that job right? Now pop your collar and make that laptop do what it does.

SERVES 1

INGREDIENTS
1   medium apple, cored and sliced into wedges
1   medium banana, sliced
1   bunch of grapes
2   Tbsp honey
3   Tbsp peanut butter

1. Spread the apple, banana, and grapes on a plate.

2. Drizzle with honey and dip whatever you're feeling into the peanut butter.

Get That Bread Sub

Is it a sub, a hoagie, a hero, or a po'boy? When you get around the country, like yours truly, it really all depends on what city the show is in that night. But when you throw some salami, provolone, and spicy peppers on it, it's for sure got that gangsta appeal. I eat this when I'm on some straight business mode, "you ain't tellin' me; I'm tellin' you" type of thang. But before you keep it way too G, make sure you got the right kind of roll, neffew. Like the older homies hustling on the block used to tell me when I was just a young pup: "It's all about that bread." Don't trip if your meats ain't on Don Corleone level—as long as you got a combo of some hard and spicy, soft and buttery cuts and a fresh roll, you'll end up with a sandwich worthy of any wise guy.

SERVES 2

FOR THE SUB:

1   16-in [40.5-cm] Italian roll or two 8-in [20-cm] Italian rolls, split
    Mayonnaise (optional)
4   slices mortadella or bologna
6   slices hot coppa
6   slices soppressata
6   slices salami
8   slices provolone cheese

FOR THE TOPPINGS:
Sliced tomato
Shredded iceberg lettuce
Thinly sliced red onion
Sliced banana peppers (optional)
Extra-virgin olive oil
Red wine vinegar
Generous pinch of oregano
Salt
Cracked black pepper

TO MAKE THE SUB:

1. If using, spread some mayonnaise (a little or a lot) on the insides of the sandwich roll(s).

2. Down the middle of the roll(s), layer the mortadella, coppa, soppressata, and salami, allowing the edges to overlap and drape over the edge of the sandwich.

3. Layer on the provolone.

TO FINISH THE SUB:

1. Top with tomato, lettuce, red onion, and banana peppers (if using).

2. Sprinkle with olive oil and red wine vinegar just the way you like it. Add a generous pinch of oregano and season with salt and pepper. Serve immediately, if you can wait that long.

06
Fried Bologna Sandwich

1. BOLOGNA

2. WHITE BREAD

3. YELLOW MUSTARD

4. AMERICAN CHEESE

5. BARBECUE POTATO CHIPS

Now this is a certified hood classic. When I was a young'in in need of something to snack on, I could count on the fridge to hold me down with some leftover cold cuts. A favorite munchie was discovered when I had the bright idea of throwing that bologna in a frying pan. Fry that Oscar Meyer up with some cheese and you're on your way to a bomb meal, Jack! But now that we moved on up, like *The Jeffersons*, that bologna turned into the finest aged meats. We ain't eating this just cuz we have to. These days we eat it because what would go better with that thang we love to do so much. Maybe I'll start making it with some "smoked" Gouda now. Get the picture?

SERVES 1

INGREDIENTS

3 slices bologna
1 Tbsp unsalted butter
2 slices white bread
1 tsp yellow mustard
3 slices American cheese
Barbecue potato chips, as many as you want

1. Place the bologna on a cutting board and cut one slit from the middle to the edge of each slice.

2. In a medium skillet over medium heat, melt the butter. Swirl the skillet to cover the bottom completely. When the skillet is hot and the foam has subsided, add the bread. Lightly toast for about 2 minutes per side, or until golden. Transfer to a cutting board and spread the mustard on one slice of bread.

3. Return the skillet to the heat and add the bologna in a single layer. Cook for 2 to 3 minutes, or until the edges are golden and crisp. Flip the bologna and top each slice with the American cheese. Cook for 2 to 3 minutes more, or until the cheese starts to melt.

4. Place the fried bologna and cheese on the toasted bread slice without mustard and top with as many chips as you and your sandwich can handle.

5. Close the sandwich, placing the other bread slice, mustard-side down, on top. Go to town.

MISSIS-SIPPI SIPPI CATFISH SANDWICH

SERVES
4

This one right here reminds me of visiting the family down in Mississippi. When I sit down with my folks there, you can bet there's some **CATFISH** on the dinner table and some **HUSH PUPPIES** on the side. It's been that way for as long as I can remember. Damn near everyone in the **HOOD** in Cali got grandparents that moved to the Golden State from somewhere in the South. Matter of fact, that's where we all started off at.

Trust me, we got that fried fish over here, too. When you in Mississippi eating that catfish and hush puppies though, it's like you're tapped in to a time long before. Over the years, many music journalists have commented that I seem to have an **OLD SOUL**—somehow connected to the past. Well, if they seen me sitting up in my family's yard eating a **CATFISH SANDWICH**, doused with hot sauce, they would damn sure know why.

TARTAR SAUCE

- ½ cup [120 g] mayonnaise
- 2 Tbsp finely diced bread-and-butter pickles
- 1 Tbsp finely chopped fresh dill
- 2 tsp bread-and-butter pickle brine
  Salt
  Cracked black pepper

CATFISH SANDWICHES

- ¾ cup [105 g] all-purpose flour
- ¾ cup [105 g] finely ground cornmeal
- ¼ tsp cayenne pepper
- 2 large eggs, beaten
  Salt
  Cracked black pepper
- 2 8-oz [230 g] catfish fillets, halved
  Vegetable oil, for frying
- 4 soft white sandwich rolls
- 4 romaine lettuce leaves
  Hot sauce for serving (optional)

TO MAKE THE

TARTAR SAUCE

In a small bowl, stir together the mayonnaise, pickles, dill, and pickle brine. Season with salt and pepper. Stir again to combine.

Cover and refrigerate until ready to use.

CATFISH SANDWICHES

 Place the flour into a shallow bowl. Place the cornmeal and cayenne into another shallow bowl; whisk to combine. Place the eggs into a third shallow bowl. Season each bowl with salt and pepper and whisk to combine.

 One at a time, dredge the catfish fillets in the flour, dip into the egg, letting the excess drip back into the bowl, and coat with the corn-meal mixture. Set aside.

 In a heavy-bottomed pot or deep fryer over high heat, heat 3 in [7.5 cm] of vegetable oil to 375°F [190°C]. Line a plate with paper towels and set aside.

 Carefully add the fish to the hot oil. Fry for 5 to 7 minutes, turning once about halfway through the cooking time, until golden brown all over. Transfer the cooked fish to the prepared plate to drain.

 Toast the sandwich rolls, if that's how you like them, and spread tartar sauce on both cut sides of each roll. Assemble each sand-wich with 1 piece of catfish and 1 lettuce leaf. Serve immediately, doused with hot sauce, if you like.

Caribbean Queen Cubano

Miami is not only the home turf of the homies Rick Ross, DJ Khaled, and Uncle Luke, but also to some of the baddest clubs I've been to. It's like Puffy is throwing a party there every damn weekend. That place ain't like nowhere else in the States. The Latin flavor is so heavy, the islands are in effect, and the vibe is real sexy. I love getting in one of those old schools and driving around South Beach or Star Island like a real boss player. But it ain't all about the women and the weather bro bro. When in Rome, you better do it how they do it. And from the Colombianos to the Dominicanos and the Puerto Ricans to the Haitians and Jamaicans, you just ain't gonna get that food flavor nowhere else. And nothing says Miami flavor better than an old-fashioned Cubano sandwich. It's heavy on the ham and all gas on the flavor. If you ain't got any shredded pork on deck, better double up on that ham. Yeah, double your pleasure, double your fun. Why not, not why?

SERVES 2

INGREDIENTS

2   Tbsp pickle brine, plus 2
    dill pickles, sliced

2   crusty soft rolls, split
    Yellow mustard
    Mayonnaise

8   slices Swiss cheese

8   thick slices ham (Black
    Forest works well)

2   cups leftover roasted
    shredded pork

4   Tbsp [55 g] unsalted
    butter, plus more for
    spreading

1. Sprinkle the pickle brine on the insides of the sandwich rolls.

2. Spread the insides of the rolls with a thin layer of mustard and mayonnaise.

3. Lay 2 Swiss cheese slices on both sides of each roll. Top the cheese evenly with pickles on both sides.

4. Lay 2 ham slices on both sides of each roll. Top the ham evenly on each roll, on one side only, with 1 cup of pork. Press both sides of each sandwich together. Spread the top of each sandwich with a thin layer of butter.

5. In a large skillet over medium heat, melt 4 Tbsp [55 g] of butter. Swirl the skillet to cover the bottom completely.

6. When the skillet is hot and the foam has subsided, add the sandwiches. Place a clean cast iron skillet on top of the sandwiches, or use a large weighted plate (you want to press the sandwiches down evenly to flatten them). Cook for 3 to 4 minutes. Lift the edge of the sandwich with a spatula to check that the bottom is golden brown and crisp and the cheese is completely melted. Flip and cook for 3 to 4 minutes more, checking again.

7. Remove the sandwiches from the skillet, cut in half, and serve immediately.

No Limit Po' Boy

When you down in the Big Easy, them long sandwiches are called po' boys. And I've spent many a day down in Louisiana. Shout out to the No Limit general Master P. The big homie taught me how to handle the "business" in "show business" and soon I became the biggest fish, even in a big pond. My time in Chopper City taught me that the shrimp ain't just for dippin. You can throw it on a hoagie, with a little mayonnaise and, if you can make it like Big ol' Snoopy D-O-double-G, it just might make 'em say uhh (uhh), Na-nah na-nah (na-nah na-nah). This taste really has No Limit.

SERVES 4

FOR THE SHRIMP:
1 cup [140 g] all-purpose flour
1 cup [140 g] yellow cornmeal
1 tsp cayenne pepper
1 tsp garlic powder
  Salt
  Cracked black pepper
1 cup [240 ml] buttermilk
1 lb shrimp, peeled and deveined
  Canola oil, for frying

FOR THE PO' BOYS:
4 crusty white sandwich rolls, split
  Mayonnaise
  Hot sauce
1 medium tomato, sliced
1 cup [45 g] shredded iceberg lettuce
  Pickle relish, for serving

TO BATTER THE SHRIMP:
1. In a large bowl, stir together the flour, cornmeal, cayenne, and garlic powder. Season with salt and pepper. Stir again to combine. Transfer to a large shallow dish. Place another large shallow dish next to the flour mixture and add the buttermilk to it. Place a wire rack or pan next to the two dishes; this will be where you set your battered shrimp.

2. Toss the shrimp fully in the buttermilk. Working with about a handful of shrimp at a time, lift the shrimp out of the buttermilk and let any excess drip back into the dish. Dredge the shrimp in the flour mixture, coating each shrimp completely. Place the battered shrimp on the wire rack or pan and repeat with the remaining shrimp. Set aside.

TO FRY THE SHRIMP:
1. In a deep skillet over high heat, heat 2 in [5 cm] of canola oil to 350°F [190°C]. Set a wire rack over a plate or line a pan with brown paper and set aside.

2. Working in batches, carefully add the shrimp to the hot oil, careful not to crowd, otherwise they'll become greasy.

3. Fry the shrimp for 3 to 4 minutes, until golden brown all over. Once the shrimp are done, using a large slotted spoon or spider, transfer the shrimp to the prepared rack or pan to drain.

TO MAKE THE PO' BOYS:
1. Toast the sandwich rolls, if you like them toasted.

2. Spread mayonnaise and hot sauce on both cut sides of each roll.

3. Assemble each sandwich with fried shrimp, tomato, and lettuce. Serve immediately with pickle relish and extra hot sauce.

OG MUNCHIES
*
CHIP ROUNDUP

~ 1 ~

LAY'S BARBECUE POTATO CHIPS

And it don't stop. These barbecue potato chips are the fancier version of the cheap ones we used to eat from the corner store. But trust they get the job done. If you're nice with it, you can crumble these up and coat your fried chicken wings.

~ 2 ~
FRITO'S HONEY BBQ FLAVOR TWISTS

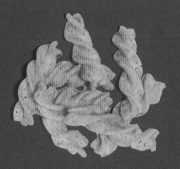

The ultimate snack. The barbecue flavor is off the hook and the twists are real crunchy. I can never have just a handful or two—it's gotta be four or five, or the entire bag.

~ 3 ~
PRINGLES

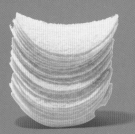

Ain't nuthin' like an OG chip. Long before they had a million different flavors, Pringles was putting their super salt in the game via a can. I dig how they did it so different with their delivery. The empty cans were also a good place to store that extra paper-bag money. So y'all know what I'm talking about.

~ 4 ~
FLAMIN' HOT CHEETOS

You already know. The hood staple. Every ghetto USA. But just like my guy Darius asked on that TV show *Atlanta*, "What flavor is a Flamin' Hot Cheeto?" Enquiring minds wanna know!

~ 5 ~
CHIPS AND SALSA

We in Cali with the Mexicans rolling deep. So we eatin' tacos and all of that right with these homies. They put us up on game and, every time we get the munchies, we giving it up!

CHAPTER 3

Dinner

The Last Meal Shrimp Alfredo [67]

Spaghetti de la Hood [68]

Mack and Cheese [70]   Tha Next Level

Salmon [72]   Down Under Lobster

Thermidor [74]   Yardie Yardbird [78]

Get Tha Chip Fried Chicken Wings [80]

OG Chicken and Waffles [83]

Faux-tisserie Chicken with

Vegetables [88]   Orange (but really kinda

burgundy) Chicken with White Rice [90]

Pork Chop Shop with Sweet Potato

Mash and Spinach [92]   Tha

Soft Touch Tacos [94]   Seared Filet

Mignon [97]   Baby Got Back Ribs [98]

Dirty South Gumbo [100]

GROWING UP AS a kid on the Eastside of the LBC, I knew a thing or two about a cheap dinner. We were a long way from surf 'n' turf but my Momma always knew how to rustle up some soul food that would keep us full. Years later, when me and the homies Warren G and Nate Dogg were working on our demo tape, we used to hustle up a few dollars so we could split a meal from Popeyes. Given my history in the game, it's only right that I provided a few recipes for the baller on a budget. Of course, nowadays there are times when I gotta eat like a Don. When I watch my favorite gangster movies, the kingpins are always eating on some real tip-top, drip-drop entrées. I'm talking seared steak, fresh lobster, you name it. To keep it balanced, I also provided a couple fine-dining options I enjoy when I'm in my Don Doggy zone.

The Last Meal Shrimp Alfredo

Don't even trip. I know this dish may share its name with that mark ass side switcher Fredo in *The Godfather*. But when it's time to chow down like a boss, we keeping Tha Doggfather's dinner table straight sucka free. When you pull in the team for a sit down, you gotta make sure the wine don't stop pouring and the food's just as heavy as the Gs in the room. So pull up a chair, tuck in your bib, and take a seat. We gonna be here for a while.

SERVES 4 TO 6

INGREDIENTS

1   tsp salt, plus more for salting the water
1   lb [455 g] linguine or fettuccine
1   lemon
4   Tbsp [55 g] unsalted butter
4   garlic cloves, smashed
1   lb [455 g] shrimp, peeled and deveined
1¾ cups [420 ml] heavy cream
1   cup [30g] ground or finely grated Parmesan cheese, plus more for serving
    Cracked black pepper

1. Bring a large pot of heavily salted water to a boil over high heat. Add the pasta. Cook until al dente, about 1 minute less than the package instructions. Drain and return the pasta to the pot.

2. While the pasta cooks, using a rasp-style grater, remove the lemon zest and set the zest aside. Slice the lemon into ¼-in [6-mm] rounds and pick out any visible seeds.

3. In a large skillet over medium-high heat, melt the butter. Swirl the skillet to cover the bottom completely.

4. When the skillet is hot and the foam has subsided, add the garlic and lemon slices. Cook for about 5 minutes, stirring occasionally, until lightly browned and fragrant.

5. Add the shrimp. Cook for 2 to 3 minutes, stirring constantly, until just firm. Remove the skillet from the heat. Using a slotted spoon or tongs, transfer the shrimp to a plate. Discard the lemon and garlic, leaving as much of the butter and juices in the skillet as possible.

6. Place the skillet over low heat. Add the cream and 1 tsp of salt. Bring to a simmer. Cook for 4 to 6 minutes until reduced.

7. Stir in the cooked shrimp, Parmesan cheese, and lemon zest. Scrape the contents of the skillet into the pot with the cooked pasta and stir well to combine. Serve immediately, seasoned with plenty of pepper and topped with additional Parmesan, as desired.

Spaghetti de la Hood

Dig this—we make spaghetti and meatballs a little different in the hood. Some of y'all like to prepare the pasta, carefully pour over the sauce, and craft a few huge meatballs to throw on top. We ain't got time for all that: Just throw everything in the pot and taste how good it is when you mix it all together. From NYC to the LBC, if you're in the hood, that's how we make it. Sprinkle a little cheese on top and you're good to go. So says Chef Boyar-Dogg!

SERVES 4

INGREDIENTS

1   lb [455 g] ground sirloin
1   cup [140 g] dry Italian bread crumbs
1   Tbsp chopped fresh parsley
1   Tbsp grated Parmesan cheese, plus more for serving
2   tsp salt, plus more for salting the water
½   tsp cracked black pepper
1   large egg, beaten
¼   cup [60 ml] olive oil
1   cup [140 g] chopped onion
4   garlic cloves, chopped
2   28-oz [800-g] cans whole peeled tomatoes
1   tsp granulated sugar
1   bay leaf
1   6-oz [170 g] can tomato paste
1   lb [455 g] spaghetti

1. In a large bowl, combine the ground sirloin, bread crumbs, parsley, Parmesan, salt, pepper, and beaten egg. Mix well to combine the ingredients. Form the meat mixture into 12 ping-pong size balls. Set aside.

2. Place a large Dutch oven over medium heat. When the pot is hot, add the meatballs, being careful not to crowd them. Cook for 7 to 8 minutes, turning occasionally, until browned. Using a slotted spoon, transfer the meatballs to a plate. Discard the grease in the pot.

3. Return the pot to medium heat and add the olive oil. Swirl the pot to coat the bottom completely.

4. Once the pot is hot, add the onion and garlic. Sauté for 4 to 5 minutes until the onion is translucent. Stir in the tomatoes, sugar, and bay leaf. Taste and adjust the salt, as needed. Cover the pot and turn the heat to low. Simmer for 30 minutes.

5. Stir in the tomato paste. Add the meatballs. Return the mixture to a simmer. Cover the pot and cook for 30 minutes more.

6. While the sauce cooks, bring a large pot of heavily salted water to a boil over high heat. Add the pasta. Cook until al dente, about 1 minute less than the package instructions. Drain the spaghetti and add it to the pot with the meatballs and sauce. Gently stir to coat the pasta in the sauce.

7. Serve the spaghetti and meatballs with a side of garlic bread, if desired.

MACK and CHEESE

SERVES
4 TO 6

Another Southern staple. If you in a soul food spot and they're not serving up some real thick, real cheesy mac, you messed up somewhere and might as well dip. Shout out to Edna Lewis for helping to get **OUR** food into these types of cookbooks. Ya know, the stuff that **WE** eat on.

Now, there's classic mac and cheese, and then there's Boss Lady's **MACK AND CHEESE**. Yeah, this right here was inspired by my wife Shante Broadus, a.k.a. **"THE BOSS LADY."** She knows that the way to a Dogg's heart is through his stomach, so she's making enough of this cheesy treat to keep **THE DOGG** always comin' back for more. She just knows my flavor and what to do to make it taste just the way I like it. Betcha can't do it like she do. What's so special about my baby's Mack and Cheese? Simple, it's just like Carlton from *The Fresh Prince of Bel Air*, it's **CHEESY** as a mofo.

2	tsp salt, plus more for salting the water		4	Tbsp [55 g] unsalted butter
1	lb [455 g] elbow macaroni		¼	cup [35 g] all-purpose flour
2	cups [480 ml] whole milk		⅔	cup [80 g] sour cream
1	cup [240 ml] heavy cream		1	tsp cracked black pepper
4	Tbsp [55 g] unsalted butter		2	tsp dry mustard
¼	cup [35 g] all-purpose flour		½	tsp ground nutmeg
5	cups [400 g] shredded extra-sharp Cheddar cheese		2	tsp Worcestershire sauce
			¼	tsp cayenne pepper

1. Preheat the oven to 400°F [200°C], with a rack in the middle position. Lightly butter a 9-by-13-in [23-by-33-cm] baking dish and set aside.

2. Bring a large pot of heavily salted water to a boil. Add the macaroni and cook until al dente, about 1 minute less than the package instructions. Drain and set aside.

3. In a small saucepan over medium heat, heat the milk and cream, being careful not to boil it.

4. While the milk heats, in a large skillet over medium heat, melt the butter. Sprinkle in the flour and whisk constantly for 2 to 3 minutes. Gradually whisk in the warmed milk. Cook for 2 minutes, whisking frequently, or until thickened and smooth. (Adjust the heat to keep the milk from boiling).

5. Gradually add 2½ cups [200 g] of the shredded cheese, whisking until fully incorporated and smooth. Add the sour cream and whisk until smooth. Add the pepper, dry mustard, cayenne, and Worcestershire sauce. Season with salt.

6. Add the cooked macaroni to the cheese sauce and stir until combined. Spoon the mixture into the prepared baking dish. Top evenly with the remaining 2½ cups [200 g] of cheese. Bake for 25 to 30 minutes, or until golden and bubbly. Serve warm.

7. If you're not serving it the same day, the Mack and Cheese can be kept, covered in the refrigerator, for up to 3 days, or in plastic wrap and aluminum foil in the freezer for up to 2 months.

Tha Next Level Salmon

Let's be honest. These days, salmon ain't really that special. It's become almost a little drowned out, don't you think? What used to be a real marker of some next level sophisticated-ness just ain't really all that awe inspiring. So when you stuck with a fillet of that passé pescado, that's when you call in Uncle Snoopy to get ya right. Just some honey mustard and your gonna blast off far above basic. I find that some greens usually set the whole meal off—nah, not my usual green "herbs," but a pan of some green beans. No more swimming upstream to make your dinner dance, now you're going with the flow neff. Ooh-wee...

SERVES 4

FOR THE SALMON:

3   Tbsp Dijon mustard
1   Tbsp honey
2   tsp white wine vinegar
4   4- to 6-oz [115- to 170-
    g] center-cut skinless
    salmon fillets (about 1½
    in or 4 cm, thick)
    Salt
    Cracked black pepper
1   Tbsp finely chopped
    fresh parsley

FOR THE GREEN BEANS:

12 oz [340 g] green beans,
    trimmed
2   garlic cloves, thinly
    sliced
2   Tbsp olive oil or vegeta-
    ble oil
    Salt
    Cracked black pepper

TO MAKE THE SALMON:

1. Preheat the oven to 425°F
    [220°C], with a rack in the
    middle position. Line a
    rimmed baking sheet with
    parchment paper or alumi-
    num foil and set aside.

2. In a large bowl, stir
    together the mustard,
    honey, and vinegar until
    smooth.

3. Season the salmon fillets
    all over with salt and
    pepper. Add them to the
    bowl and toss with the
    sauce until evenly coated.
    Transfer the fillets to the
    prepared baking sheet
    and arrange them in a row
    along one short side of the
    sheet. Drizzle the sauce
    left in the bowl over the
    fillets.

**TO MAKE THE GREEN
BEANS:**

1. In a medium bowl, com-
    bine the green beans and
    garlic. Drizzle with the olive
    oil and toss until evenly
    coated. Spread the beans
    in a single layer on the
    remaining space left on
    the baking sheet. Season
    with salt and pepper.

2. Place the sheet in the
    oven and bake until the
    green beans are tender
    and golden brown at the
    edges, and the salmon
    is lightly browned on the
    outside and cooked on the
    inside, 10 to 14 minutes,
    depending on how well
    you like your salmon
    cooked (10 minutes for
    medium; 12 minutes for
    medium-well; 14 minutes
    for well).

3. Remove the baking sheet
    from the oven. Divide the
    salmon and green beans
    among four serving plates
    and sprinkle with the pars-
    ley before serving.

Down Under Lobster Thermidor

First time I had this I was in Australia. I usually go out there like once a year. This time we had a big tour that we went on. Like a big, big tour. Bow Wow, Nelly, Fat Joe, The Game, Busta Rhymes, Ciara—it was just a whole host of people out there. We was at the Versace Hotel, a seven-star place where everything is Versace: the glass, the floors, the ashtrays, the towels, the socks, the robes, the mirrors—everything is all Versace. It's one of those hotels where you know it ain't for everybody; you gotta be somebody.

So, we had ordered some regular room service but then the chef was telling me about something that I should try, Lobster Thermidor. And, I'm like, alright bring it on up. I'm telling you neffew, that shit was so good. When I got back to the States, I was trying to figure out where I could get it at. But when I found it here, it didn't taste like the one in Australia. So in true Boss Dogg fashion, I did it myself and added my own flavor to give it the taste that I was looking for. And after I tried it a few times, I mastered the plan on how to make it taste like the way I wanted it to taste. I served it to a few people and it became one of my biggest and best dishes. From me to you...enjoy!

THA FLIP

I like to serve the lobster claws whole so we can all get it crackin' together with that extra meat and wild out at the dinner table.

SERVES 6

INGREDIENTS

3   1¼-lb [570-g] lobsters
4   Tbsp [55 g] unsalted butter
3   garlic cloves, chopped
2   shallots, chopped
¼   cup [35 g] all-purpose flour
⅓   cup [80 ml] dry white wine
1   tsp dry mustard
2   cups [480 ml] heavy cream
1   tsp salt
½   tsp cracked black pepper
1   cup [80 g] shredded Gruyère cheese
1   cup [30 g] grated Parmesan cheese
¾   cup [60 g] crushed butter crackers
¼   cup [10 g] chopped flat-leaf parsley leaves
½   cup [50 g] chopped scallion, white and light green parts

1. Fill a large bowl with ice and water and set aside. Line a baking sheet with aluminum foil and set aside.

2. Fill a large stockpot three-fourths full with water. Place it over high heat and bring to a boil. Add the lobsters. Cook for 8 to 10 minutes until they turn red. Transfer the lobsters to the ice bath to stop the cooking.

3. When cool enough to handle, using a sharp knife, halve the lobsters lengthwise. Remove the meat and place it in a small bowl. Remove and discard the innards. Rinse the lobster shells and place on the prepared baking sheet. Set aside.

4. Preheat the broiler, with a rack in the middle position.

5. In a skillet over medium heat, melt the butter. Swirl the skillet to cover the bottom completely.

6. When the skillet is hot and the foam has subsided, add the garlic and shallots. Cook for 30 seconds. Gradually add the flour

and whisk to combine. Cook for about 2 minutes, whisking until the mixture is thick and pale yellow. Whisk in the wine, mustard, cream, salt, and pepper until smooth.

7. Stir in the Gruyère and Parmesan cheeses until melted and thick. Stir in the lobster meat until just coated. Remove from the heat. Divide the mixture among the lobster shells. Sprinkle the top of each lobster with crushed crackers.

8. Place the lobsters under the broiler for 4 to 5 minutes until the tops are golden brown. Garnish with the parsley and scallion. Serve warm.

Yardie Yardbird

From Dogg to Lion...One of the best parts about traveling to Jamaica to record my reggae album *Reincarnated* was getting to indulge in some *real* jerk chicken. Sometimes that thang be so hot that it'll catch up with you a few minutes after you dig in. The chicken my Jamaican homies cooked up was so fire that you know Tha Bigg Boss Dogg had to get his paws on the recipe. And I got something that will wash all that jerk down perfectly. I bet it ain't hard to guess what that is. Jah!

SERVES 4

FOR THE JERK MARINADE:

¼ cup [60 ml] olive oil

2 Tbsp molasses

2 Tbsp freshly squeezed lime juice

2 habanero peppers, stemmed and seeded

6 scallions, white and light green parts, roughly chopped

1 1-in [2.5-cm] piece peeled fresh ginger

6 garlic cloves, peeled

1 Tbsp dried thyme leaves

1 tsp ground allspice

1 tsp salt

1 tsp cracked black pepper

1 3½-lb [1.6 kg] whole chicken, cut into 8 pieces (2 wings, 2 legs, 2 breasts, 2 thighs)

Cooked white rice, for serving

2 limes, halved

TO MAKE THE JERK MARINADE:

1. In a food processor, combine the olive oil, molasses, lime juice, habaneros, scallions, ginger, garlic, thyme, allspice, salt, and pepper. Process until smooth. The mixture should be thick.

2. Put the chicken into a large ziplock bag, or a large bowl. Pour the marinade over the chicken. Seal the bag and manipulate the chicken to coat it in the marinade. Or, using your clean hands, toss the chicken pieces in the bowl to coat in the marinade and cover the bowl with plastic wrap. Refrigerate the chicken to marinate for 1 hour, and up to overnight.

TO MAKE THE CHICKEN:

1. Preheat the oven to 375°F [190°C], with a rack in the middle position.

2. Transfer the chicken and marinade to a large roasting pan. Place the pan in the oven and bake for 45 to 55 minutes until the chicken is glazed and dark brown. Check the wings and legs first for doneness, followed by the thighs and the breasts: An instant-read thermometer inserted into the chicken (not touching the bone) should read at least 165°F [75°C].

3. Remove the chicken from the oven and let rest for 10 minutes.

4. Serve over cooked white rice with the lime halves for squeezing.

DINNER

Get Tha Chip Fried Chicken Wings

My cousin MacShawn 100 is from the Bay Area. He's just a ball of energy and he gives you a whole lot of laughs. So he comes out on the road with me and the team a lot. This one time we had did a show and they had some food in the back, but the chicken wings didn't have no flavor on them. So MacShawn was like, "Man, hand me them potato chips." So he threw a couple of wings in the bag, shook them up, took a bite—and he was like, "Taste this shit, neffew!"

So when I got home, I fried some chicken and put some potato chips in the batter. And when I did that, man, my whole family was touched by the meal. Lay's Barbecue or Lay's Sour Cream. It's Snoop's shake and bake. From me to you.

SERVES 6
MAKES 28 TO 30 WINGS

FOR THE BRINE:
- ⅓ cup [65 g] granulated sugar
- ⅓ cup [55 g] kosher salt
- 1 bay leaf
- 1 tsp red pepper flakes
  Peel of 1 orange

FOR THE CHICKEN:
- 4 lb [1.8 kg] chicken wings
- 2 cups [280 g] all-purpose flour
- ¼ cup [35 g] cornmeal
- ¼ cup [14 g] crushed potato chips
- 2 tsp garlic powder
- 1 tsp cayenne pepper
- ½ tsp baking powder
- 2 tsp cracked black pepper
- 2 tsp salt, plus more for seasoning
- 2 cups [480 ml] buttermilk
- 1 qt [960 ml] canola oil
  Lemon pepper, for serving (optional)
  Hot sauce, for serving (optional)

CONTINUED

TO BRINE THE CHICKEN:

1. Fill a large pot with 5 cups [1.2 L] of water. Place the pot over high heat and bring to a boil. Add the sugar, salt, bay leaf, red pepper flakes, and orange peel. Cook, stirring, until the sugar and salt dissolve, about 1 minute. Remove from the heat and let cool.

2. Place the chicken in a large bowl and cover completely with the cooled brine. Cover and refrigerate for 10 to 12 hours, and up to 24 hours.

3. Remove the chicken from the brine and pat dry with a paper towel. Set the chicken aside and discard the brine.

TO BATTER THE CHICKEN:

1. In a large bowl, stir together the flour, cornmeal, crushed potato chips, garlic powder, cayenne, baking powder, black pepper, and salt until combined. Transfer to a large shallow dish. Place another large shallow dish next to the flour mixture and add the buttermilk to it. Place a wire rack or pan next to the two dishes; this will be where you set your battered chicken.

2. Take one wing and submerge it in the buttermilk. Lift and let any excess drip back into the dish. Roll the wing in the flour mixture, coating it completely. Place the battered chicken wing on the wire rack or pan and repeat with the remaining wings.

3. Let the wings dry for 20 to 30 minutes before frying.

TO FRY THE CHICKEN:

1. In a large Dutch oven over medium heat, heat the canola oil to 350°F [180°C]. Place a wire rack over a plate or line a pan with brown paper and set aside.

2. Working in batches, carefully add the chicken wings to the hot oil, careful not to crowd, otherwise they'll become greasy. Once the chicken is added, the oil's temperature will drop to between 300°F to 320°F [150°C to 160°C]. Watch and adjust the heat to maintain a consistent 350°F [180°C] temperature.

3. Fry the wings for 8 to 10 minutes, or until golden. If the chicken is getting too dark, lower the heat. Once the chicken is done, remove each piece with tongs and transfer to the prepared rack or pan to drain. Sprinkle generously with salt or lemon pepper (if using).

4. Let the oil come back to temperature before adding the next batch; repeat with the remaining chicken.

5. Serve the wings with plenty of hot sauce and lemon pepper (if using), hot or cold, however you like them.

OG Chicken and Waffles

Now, if you're gonna make these, they gotta be on par with Roscoe's in L.A. A lot of times people want to try shit at home that they get at a restaurant. This is one of those that I wanted to see if I could flip and make it work because I'm like damn near synonymous with chicken and waffles now. I tried and tried, added a little tweak here and there. And guess what? It worked. Now the real challenge here is taking time to brine and letting that battered chicken sit for 30 minutes before frying. Yeah, yeah, I know—you want it now. Ain't you ever heard that perfection takes time? The wait is worth it, and so is keeping that canola oil on deck. That oil and brine makes chicken mighty fine.

SERVES 4

FOR THE CHICKEN:

Brine recipe (see page 80)

1 3½-lb [1.6-kg] whole chicken, cut into 10 pieces (2 wings, 2 legs, 2 breasts cut crosswise, 2 thighs)

3 cups [420 g] all-purpose flour

¾ cup [105 g] yellow cornmeal

4 tsp cayenne pepper

¾ tsp baking powder

4 tsp cracked black pepper

3 tsp salt, plus more for seasoning

2 cups [480 ml] buttermilk

1 qt [960 ml] canola oil

FOR THE WAFFLES:

1¾ cups [245 g] all-purpose flour

¼ cup [50 g] granulated sugar

3 Tbsp yellow cornmeal

½ tsp baking soda

2 large eggs

2 cups [480 ml] buttermilk

1 tsp pure vanilla extract

8 Tbsp [1 stick, or 110 g] unsalted butter, melted, plus more for serving

Maple syrup, for serving

CONTINUED

OG Chicken and Waffles

TO BRINE THE CHICKEN, FOLLOW THE RECIPE AND METHOD ON PAGE 82.

TO BATTER THE CHICKEN, FOLLOW THE METHOD ON PAGE 82.

TO FRY THE CHICKEN:

1. In a large Dutch oven over medium heat, heat the canola oil to 350°F [180°C]. Set a wire rack over a plate or line a pan with brown paper and set aside.

2. Working in batches beginning with the drumsticks, carefully add the chicken to the hot oil, careful not to crowd the chicken, otherwise it'll become greasy. Once the chicken is added, the oil's temperature will drop to between 300°F to 320°F [150°C to 160°C]. Watch and adjust the heat to maintain a consistent 350°F [180°C] temperature.

3. Fry the drumsticks for about 15 minutes, or until golden. Once the chicken is done, remove each piece with tongs and transfer to the prepared rack or pan to drain. Sprinkle generously with salt.

4. Fry the breasts and thighs for about 10 minutes, or until golden. If the chicken is getting too dark, lower the heat. When done, transfer to the rack or pan. Sprinkle generously with salt.

5. Fry the wings for about 8 minutes, or until golden. When done, transfer to the rack or pan. Sprinkle generously with salt.

6. Let the chicken rest for at least 10 minutes before serving.

TO MAKE THE WAFFLES:

1. Preheat a waffle maker to 350°F [180°C].

2. In a large bowl, stir together the flour, sugar, cornmeal, and baking soda until combined. In another bowl, beat the eggs and add the buttermilk, vanilla, and melted butter. Gradually add the dry mixture to the wet until incorporated (the batter will be lumpy).

3. Following the manufacturer's instructions, pour the batter into the waffle maker and cook the waffles until golden brown.

Top each waffle with a large pat of butter. Add your favorite piece of fried chicken and pour on plenty of maple syrup.

FAUX-TISSERIE CHICKEN with VEGETABLES

SERVES
2 WITH
LEFTOVERS

Don't act like your girl really thought that rotisserie chicken you served up on your wack-ass date night didn't come directly from your local supermarket. You ain't foolin' no one but your own dumb ass. Quit acting like **FLIPPIN'** one of these birds is reserved for those in a fancy floppy chef's hat. You can do it, just like Adam Sandler in *The Waterboy*. Pop this thang out on her and now she ready to rock with ya. Like the homie MC Breed said, "**AIN'T NO FUTURE IN YOUR FRONTIN'**." Never was, cuz.

2	tsp salt	1	small yellow onion, roughly chopped
½	tsp dried thyme	2	garlic cloves
½	tsp garlic powder	1½	lb [680 g] fingerling potatoes, halved
½	tsp paprika	1	lb [455 g] carrots, cut into 1-in [2.5-cm] pieces
¼	tsp onion powder	2	Tbsp olive oil
¾	tsp cracked black pepper		
1	4-lb [1.8-kg] whole chicken, giblets removed, rinsed, and patted dry with paper towels		

1. In a small bowl, stir together 1 tsp of salt, the thyme, garlic powder, paprika, onion powder, and ½ tsp of pepper. Rub the spice mixture all over the chicken. Wrap the chicken in plastic wrap and refrigerate for at least 4 hours, but preferably overnight.

2. Preheat the oven to 275°F [135°C], with a rack in the middle position.

3. Unwrap the chicken and place it on a rimmed baking sheet. Stuff the onion and garlic into the cavity. Tie the legs together with kitchen twine.

4. Place the potatoes and carrots around the chicken on the baking sheet. Drizzle with the olive oil and sprinkle with the remaining 1 tsp of salt and ¼ tsp of pepper. Toss to coat.

5. Place the baking sheet in the oven and roast the chicken for 2½ to 3 hours, or until an instant-read thermometer inserted into the chicken thigh (not touching the bone) registers 165°F [75°C], turning the vegetables and basting the chicken every hour or so.

6. Remove the chicken and vegetables from the oven and transfer the chicken to a serving platter. Let the chicken rest for at least 10 to 15 minutes before carving, allowing the juices to distribute evenly.

7. While the chicken rests, preheat the broiler to high, with a rack directly beneath the heat source.

8. Reserve 1 Tbsp of chicken fat from the baking sheet and discard the rest. Toss the vegetables on the sheet in the reserved fat. Place them under the broiler for 3 to 5 minutes, or until golden brown, keeping a close eye to ensure the vegetables don't burn.

9. Serve the chicken with the vegetables while it's H.O.T.

Orange Chicken with White Rice

(but really kinda burgundy)

You know, here in L.A., there's always the hood Chinese places. We grew up with it. They got fried chicken and Chinese food all in the same spot. Like Louisiana chicken on the left side and Chinese food on the right side. Now I just love orange chicken from different Chinese food spots around the world. I always be asking them about the ingredients so I can put my own spin on it at home.

SERVES 4

FOR THE ORANGE SAUCE:
¾ cup [180 ml] orange juice
3 Tbsp soy sauce
1 Tbsp Sriracha
1 Tbsp honey
1 tsp sesame oil
½ tsp red pepper flakes

FOR THE CHICKEN:
2 large eggs
1½ cups [210 g] cornstarch
2 lbs [910 g] boneless skinless chicken thighs or breasts, cut into 1-in [2.5 cm] pieces
½ cup [120 ml] canola oil
Salt

Cooked white rice, for serving
2 tsp sesame seeds, for serving
2 scallions sliced, for serving

TO MAKE THE ORANGE SAUCE:

In a small saucepan over medium heat, whisk the orange juice, soy sauce, Sriracha, honey, sesame oil, and red pepper flakes. Bring to a simmer and cook for 6 to 7 minutes until thickened. Remove from the heat and set aside.

TO MAKE THE CHICKEN:

1. In a large bowl, whisk the eggs until blended. Place a large bowl next to the eggs and put the cornstarch into it.

2. Add the chicken to the bowl with the beaten egg and toss to coat. Using a spider or large slotted spoon, lift the chicken from the egg and let any excess drip back into the bowl. Toss the chicken in the cornstarch to coat, shake off any excess cornstarch, and set aside.

3. Line a plate with paper towels and set aside. In a large skillet over medium-high heat, heat the canola oil. Swirl the pan to cover the bottom completely.

4. When the skillet is hot, carefully add the chicken to the hot oil. Cook for 3 to 4 minutes on each side, or until golden and crispy. Transfer the chicken to the prepared plate and season with salt. Drain any excess oil and wipe the pan with a paper towel.

5. Return the chicken to the skillet. Pour the orange sauce over the chicken. Stir to coat. Cook for 2 to 3 minutes to heat the sauce through.

6. Serve the chicken and orange sauce over cooked white rice, garnished with sesame seeds and scallions.

Pork Chop Shop with Sweet Potato Mash and Spinach

This one is a stick-to-your-ribs must have for any comfort food connoisseur. We don't discriminate—I like lean and mean pork chops but this calls for those big, fat daddy, thick country chops. And whether you get down with some Kansas City sauce or make your own to slap on those chops really don't matter. You'll be picking that bone clean in no time fliz-at.

SERVES 4

FOR THE SWEET POTATO MASH:

4   medium sweet potatoes, peeled and cut into 1-in [2.5-cm] chunks
4   garlic cloves, peeled
5   Tbsp [70 g] unsalted butter, at room temperature
    Salt
    Cracked black pepper

FOR THE PORK CHOPS:

4   (about 1 lb [455 g] total) bone-in pork chops (1 in [2.5 cm] thick)
2   tsp sweet paprika
½   tsp cayenne pepper
    Salt
    Cracked black pepper
2   Tbsp olive oil

FOR THE BARBECUE SAUCE:

½   cup [150 g] apricot jam
¼   cup [65 g] ketchup
2   Tbsp Worcestershire sauce
2   Tbsp yellow mustard
2   Tbsp apple cider vinegar
½   tsp red pepper flakes

FOR THE SPINACH:

1   Tbsp olive oil
8   cups [160 g] loosely packed fresh baby spinach leaves
1   lemon

TO MAKE THE SWEET POTATO MASH:

In a large saucepan, combine the sweet potatoes and garlic. Cover with water and bring to a boil over high heat. Cover the pan and cook for 16 to 20 minutes until the sweet potatoes are tender, testing with a fork.

TO MAKE THE PORK CHOPS:

1. While the sweet potatoes cook, sprinkle the pork chops evenly with the paprika and cayenne. Season with salt and pepper.

2. In a large skillet over medium-high heat, heat 1 Tbsp of olive oil. Swirl the skillet to cover the bottom completely. When the skillet is hot, add two pork chops. Cook for about 4 minutes until golden. Flip and cook the other side for about 4 minutes more until golden. Remove from the skillet and tent loosely with aluminum foil to keep warm. Return the skillet to the heat and heat the remaining 1 Tbsp of olive oil. Cook the remaining two pork chops.

TO MAKE THE BARBECUE SAUCE:

1. While the pork chops cook, in a small bowl, stir together, the jam, ketchup, Worcestershire sauce, mustard, vinegar, and red pepper flakes.

2. Return the first two chops to the skillet. Pour the sauce over all the pork chops. Continue cooking for about 2 minutes more, turning the pork in the glaze as it thickens, until the pork is glazed in the sauce and cooked through. Remove the skillet from the heat and let the pork chops rest in the sauce.

TO FINISH THE SWEET POTATO MASH:

Drain the sweet potatoes and garlic in a colander and transfer to a large bowl. Reserve the saucepan. Add the butter to the sweet potatoes and mash until smooth. Season with salt and pepper.

TO MAKE THE SPINACH:

1. Wipe the reserved saucepan dry with paper towels. Add the olive oil and place the pan over medium-high heat for 1 minute.

2. Add the spinach. Cook, stirring, until slightly wilted, about 1 minute.

3. Using a rasp-style grater, grate half the lemon's zest over the spinach. Cut the lemon in half and squeeze its juice over the spinach as well. Season with salt, stir to combine, and cook for 30 seconds more. Remove the pan from the heat.

Divide the sweet potato mash among four serving plates and top each mound with a pork chop and some barbecue sauce. Spoon the spinach next to the chops and mash and serve hot.

Tha Soft Touch Tacos

You know that Tha Doggfather is as hard as they come, and can't anyone accuse me of being soft. Now soft tacos? That's a different story. Hard shell is cool but ain't nothin' like some soft flour or corn tortillas heaped with some of that prime, U.S.D.A.-approved ground beef. That's the only kind of beef I'm trying to deal with, but don't get it twisted. If you got beef with DPG, holler at me—the D-O-G-G.

SERVES 4

FOR THE FILLING:
2   Tbsp vegetable oil
1   medium onion, chopped
3   garlic cloves, chopped
1   lb [455 g] ground beef
1   tsp salt
1   tsp chili powder
1   tsp ground cumin
8   corn tortillas

FOR THE TOPPINGS:
1   cup [80 g] shredded Cheddar cheese
1   cup [45 g] shredded lettuce
8   cherry tomatoes, quartered
1   avocado, peeled, pitted, and chopped
1   jalapeño pepper, sliced
     Limes, fresh cilantro, sliced scallions, for garnishing
     Hot sauce, for serving

TO MAKE THE FILLING:

1. In a large skillet over medium-high, heat the vegetable oil. Swirl the skillet to cover the bottom completely. When the skillet is hot, add the onion. Cook for 4 to 5 minutes, stirring occasionally, until the onion is softened. Add the garlic and cook for 1 to 2 minutes more.

2. Add the ground beef, salt, chili powder, and cumin. Cook for 6 to 7 minutes, stirring often to break up the meat, until the beef is completely browned. Taste and adjust for seasoning, if necessary. Drain and discard any excess grease. Transfer the beef to a large bowl, cover, and set aside.

3. To char the tortillas, turn your gas burner to the lowest setting. Place one tortilla directly above the flame for about 45 seconds, or until the bottom is slightly crisp and charred. Using tongs, flip the tortilla, watching to make sure it doesn't burn. Place the charred tortilla on a plate and cover to keep warm. Repeat with the remaining tortillas.

TO ASSEMBLE THE TACOS:

Top each charred tortilla with beef, cheese, lettuce, tomato, avocado, and jalapeño. Garnish with lime, cilantro, scallions, and hot sauce. Serve warm.

Seared Filet Mignon

I'ma share with you one of my favorites. A simple-to-whip-up, man-food classic—filet mignon. The big time. All meat, no sweet. And while I make sure to always order a few of these bad boys when I'm staying at The W Hotel in the Big Apple, I've added a couple little twists to make it Snoop certified and official like a referee with a whistle.

But before you cook it, you should figure out how to pronounce it. Just like the gentleman you ain't.

SERVES 4

INGREDIENTS

1   Tbsp black peppercorns
1   Tbsp white peppercorns
1   Tbsp sea salt
4   10-oz [280-g] filet mignon steaks, 3 in [7.5 cm] thick
2   Tbsp unsalted butter, plus more for serving
1   Tbsp canola oil or peanut oil
1   Tbsp chopped flat-leaf parsley leaves

1. Coarsely grind the peppercorns in a spice grinder or food processor, or wrap the peppercorns in a clean dishtowel and crush them with a heavy skillet. Place the cracked pepper on a plate.

2. Season each steak on both sides with salt. Roll the steaks in the pepper until evenly coated and set aside.

3. In a large cast-iron skillet over medium-high heat, melt the butter with the oil. Swirl the skillet to cover the bottom completely.

4. When the skillet is hot and the foam has subsided, add the steaks. Sear for about 4 minutes per side, forming a dark brown crust, for medium-rare. Add an additional 2 minutes per side for medium.

5. Remove the skillet from the heat. Tent the steaks with aluminum foil and let rest for 5 minutes. Top each steak with a generous pat of butter and a sprinkle of chopped parsley and serve.

Baby Got Back Ribs

Nuthin' screams summertime in Cali like some rizibs on the grizill. And you do know that! Remember us in the classic video for "Nuthin But G Thang"? Me, Dr. Dre, and the crew holding it down at the park with the grill blazing? Or what about that classic flick with the homies Ice Cube and Cuba Gooding Jr. from *Boyz n the Hood*? Yeah, that real barbecue banger. But the weather where you stay might not be all California-fied. So I'ma show you how to get down backyard Boogie style in your own kitchen. Just remember to cook that shit slow, yo. And, oh yeah, white bread only!

SERVES 6

INGREDIENTS:

¾   cup [150 g] packed light brown sugar
1   Tbsp paprika
1   Tbsp garlic powder
1   tsp cracked black pepper
1   tsp salt
1   tsp cayenne pepper
2   racks (about 4 lb, 10 oz [2.1 kg] total) pork baby back ribs
1½   cups [430 g] barbecue sauce (Rao's or the deal from page 92)

1. Preheat the oven to 300°F [150°C], with a rack in the middle position. Line a baking sheet with two layers of aluminum foil and set aside.

2. In a small bowl, stir together the brown sugar, paprika, garlic powder, black pepper, salt, and cayenne. Apply the rub to the ribs, coating both sides. Wrap each rack in aluminum foil and place on the prepared baking sheet in a single layer.

3. Place the ribs in the oven and roast for 1½ to 2 hours, testing at 1½ hours for doneness. The meat is ready when it's tender and easy to pull away from the bone. Remove the ribs from the oven and carefully discard any pork juices from the pan. Leave the racks wrapped and set aside.

4. Preheat the broiler to its highest setting, with a rack in the top position.

5. Unwrap the ribs and brush the top side with a thick layer of barbecue sauce. Place the ribs under the broiler for about 10 minutes, or until deep brown.

6. Remove the ribs and let rest, covered, for 10 minutes. Cut the racks into 2-rib portions. Serve warm with white bread, extra barbecue sauce on the side, and lots of napkins.

Dirty South Gumbo

Now the secret to some good gumbo is throwing in a little of this and just the right amount of that. If you can't find one of these ingredients, don't be afraid to throw in a little improvisation—freestyle off the top with it. When you think something that mixed just right, look no further than Tha Dogg. Whether I'm gangsta'd out, smooth talking the ladies, inspirizing the kids as Coach Snoop, giving out dough on my very own game show, or cavorting with Ms. Martha, I make it look so tasty don't I? So take notes and get that pot popping with a whole lotta that good, good. Cuz if it tastes good to ya, it must be good for ya.

SERVES 6 TO 8

INGREDIENTS:

4   lb [1.8 kg] boneless, skinless chicken thighs
1   Tbsp Creole seasoning
2   tsp salt
1   cup [240 ml] vegetable oil
1   cup [140 g] all-purpose flour
1   large yellow onion, chopped
2   red bell peppers, chopped
4   celery stalks, roughly chopped
4   garlic cloves, peeled
8   cups [2 L] chicken stock
1½ lb [680 g] kielbasa or andouille sausage, sliced into thin rounds
2   bay leaves
⅓   cup [15 g] finely minced fresh parsley leaves
1   bunch scallions sliced, plus more for serving
¼   cup [60 ml] Louisiana hot sauce, plus more for serving
Cooked white rice, for serving

1. Season the chicken with the Creole seasoning and 1 tsp of salt. Set aside and let come to room temperature.

2. In a large Dutch oven over medium heat, warm 2 Tbsp of vegetable oil. Working in batches so as not to crowd the pan, add the chicken to the pot. Sear for 4 to 5 minutes, turning occasionally, until golden brown all over. Transfer the cooked chicken to a plate.

3. Adjust the heat under the pot to medium-low. Add the remaining vegetable oil to the Dutch oven and let warm for several minutes.

4. Whisk in the flour until thoroughly combined to form a roux. Cook the roux for 25 to 30 minutes, whisking frequently, until dark brown. It is very important that you do not let the roux burn or stick to the bottom of the pot; it will ruin the gumbo's flavor (and that would be a shame).

5. While the roux cooks, in a food processor, combine the onion, red bell peppers, celery, and garlic. Pulse until very finely minced.

6. When the roux is dark brown, add the vegetable mixture and stir to combine. Cook for 3 to 4 minutes until the vegetables are soft and the mixture is very thick. Stir in the chicken stock. Raise the heat to high to bring the mixture to a boil. Adjust the heat to maintain a simmer and scrape up any browned bits stuck to the bottom of the pot.

7. Stir in the remaining 1 tsp of salt, the sausage, bay leaves, and cooked chicken. Cover the pot and simmer the gumbo for 1 hour. Skim off any foam that rises to the surface.

8. Transfer the chicken to a cutting board and use two forks to shred it. Return the shredded chicken to the pot along with the parsley, scallions, and hot sauce. Simmer, uncovered, for 15 minutes. Taste and season with salt, as needed. Remove and discard the bay leaves.

9. Serve the hot gumbo over rice, garnished with scallions, with more hot sauce on the side.

CHAPTER 4

Dessert

Hey Auntie Banana Puddn' [105]
Rolls Royce PB-Chocolate
Chip Cookies [109] Bow Wow
Brownies and Ice Cream [110]
Buttermiziilk Pound Cake Cake
Cake Cake [112] Rags to Riches
Apple Pie [115] Gimme S'mores
Pie [118] Dipped and Whipped
Strawberries [120] Go Shorty,
It's Your Birthday Cake [123]
Hustle Hard Chocolate
Cheesecake [126]

IF YOU DON'T KNOW, you won't know: Snoop Dogg has a sweet tooth. Now it might be something to do with all the "medicine" I be chiefin' on, but that sweet tooth has a tendency to hit during the late-night hours. That's when I find myself creeping to the fridge to look for that last slice of pie, or for one more of those homemade cookies. When you go as hard as the Boss Dogg goes, sometimes you just need that sugar boost to keep you going. Well, these desserts don't skimp on the chocolate, the frosting, or the marshmallows, and they're all the better for it. Give in to a li'l temptation and try a few for yourself.

Hey Auntie Banana Puddn'

Who says fruit can't be tasty? Yeah, you could just have a regular old banana, or you could really get it crackin' with this banana pudding recipe.

SERVES 4 TO 6

FOR THE BANANA PUDDING:

1   cup [200 g] granulated sugar
¼   cup [35 g] cornstarch
¾   tsp salt
2   cups [480 ml] whole milk
1¼   cups [300 ml] heavy cream
1   large egg, lightly beaten
1   Tbsp pure vanilla extract
4   medium bananas

½   box [5½ oz, or 155 g] Nilla wafers, or other small vanilla cookies

FOR THE RUM WHIPPED CREAM:

1   cup [240 ml] heavy cream
2   Tbsp confectioners' sugar
3   Tbsp dark rum (optional)
½   tsp pure vanilla extract

TO MAKE THE BANANA PUDDING:

1. In a medium saucepan, whisk the sugar, cornstarch, and salt. Add the milk and cream and whisk again to blend.

2. Add the egg and place the saucepan over medium-high heat. Whisking constantly, cook until the mixture begins to thicken and bubbles begin popping on the surface. Decrease the heat to medium and whisk vigorously for 45 seconds. Remove the pan from the heat.

CONTINUED

3. Strain the pudding through a fine-mesh sieve into a heat-proof bowl. Add the vanilla and whisk until incorporated. Place a piece of plastic wrap directly onto the pudding's surface. Refrigerate until chilled, 2 to 4 hours, stirring occasionally.

4. Whisk the chilled pudding to loosen. Chop 2 bananas into cubes. Fold the banana cubes into the chilled pudding. Slice the remaining 2 bananas into rounds, setting aside one banana slice for each glass for garnishing.

5. Place 1 or 2 Tbsp of pudding into the bottom of a 6-oz [180-ml] glass. Add a layer of sliced bananas and top with a layer of vanilla wafers, breaking them, if necessary, so you have a solid layer of wafers. Repeat the layers until you reach the top of the glass, ending with a layer of pudding. Continue with the remaining ingredients to fill the other glasses. Refrigerate for at least 4 hours.

TO MAKE THE RUM WHIPPED CREAM:

1. Refrigerate the bowl of a stand mixer and the whisk attachment, or a medium metal bowl and the beaters of a handheld electric mixer, for about 15 minutes until quite cold.

2. Once chilled, remove the bowl and whisk from the refrigerator. Add the cream. Whip on medium speed until just thickened.

3. Add the confectioners' sugar, rum (if using), and vanilla. Whip again, on medium-high speed, until the cream holds soft peaks. Top each pudding with a dollop of whipped cream and place a banana slice decoratively on top. Serve immediately.

4. The puddings will keep, refrigerated and lightly covered in plastic wrap, for a day or so, but are best the day they are made.

Rolls Royce PB–Chocolate Chip Cookies

Everybody knows my man Berner got the best cookies in the land. Thing is, the cookies he's slanging are for smoking, not for eating. If you're looking for more of a chocolate chip, peanut butter kind of thing, this recipe will leave you highly satisfied.

MAKES 3 DOZEN

INGREDIENTS

1½	cups [210 g] all-purpose flour
1	tsp baking soda
½	tsp salt
16	Tbsp [2 sticks, or 220 g] unsalted butter, at room temperature
½	cup [130 g] creamy peanut butter
½	cup [100 g] packed light brown sugar
½	cup [100 g] granulated sugar
1	large egg
1	tsp pure vanilla extract
2	cups [360 g] semisweet chocolate morsels

1. Preheat the oven to 375°F [190°C], with one rack in the upper third and one in the lower third of the oven. Line two baking sheets with parchment paper and set aside.

2. In a small bowl, stir together the flour, baking soda, and salt.

3. In a large bowl, combine the butter, peanut butter, brown sugar, and granulated sugar. Using a handheld electric mixer on medium speed, or a wooden spoon, vigorously beat the mixture until smooth.

4. Stir in the egg and vanilla.

5. Gradually stir in the flour mixture just until combined. Stir in the chocolate morsels. Using a tablespoon, drop rounded dough portions onto the prepared baking sheets, about 2 in [5 cm] apart.

6. Place one sheet on the upper rack and one on the lower; bake for 8 to 10 minutes until golden, switching the sheets top to bottom and front to back halfway through the baking time to ensure even baking.

7. Remove the cookies from the oven and let cool on the sheets for 5 minutes. Transfer the cookies to a wire rack to cool completely.

8. Store the cooled cookies at room temperature in an airtight container or ziplock bag for up to 3 days.

Bow Wow Brownies and Ice Cream

My greatest recipe is Bow Wow Brownies. The key is to make sure they're nicely baked. If I really want to take it up a notch, I might even add a dash of my secret ingredient—a sprinkle of Snoop's herbs and spices really gives those things a kick. They'll come out the oven smelling real aromatic, and a couple bites will leave you feeling like you're on cloud nine. This is why you bought the book right? So what the hell you waiting on? Go get baked!

SERVES 6

INGREDIENTS

⅔ cup [90 g] all-purpose flour
¼ tsp baking soda
½ tsp salt
½ cup [100 g] granulated sugar
3 Tbsp unsalted butter
2 Tbsp whole milk
2½ cups [450 g] milk chocolate morsels
2 large eggs
½ tsp pure vanilla extract
Your favorite vanilla ice cream, for serving
Chocolate sauce, for serving

1. Preheat the oven to 325°F [165°C], with a rack in the middle position. Butter an 8-by-8-in [20-by-20-cm] square baking pan and set aside.

2. In a small bowl, whisk the flour, baking soda, and salt. Set aside.

3. In a medium saucepan over medium heat, combine the sugar, butter, and milk. Bring to a boil. Remove the pan from the heat and add 1½ cups [270 g] of the chocolate morsels. Stir until the chocolate is melted and smooth.

4. Add the eggs and vanilla to the chocolate. Stir until blended and smooth.

5. Gradually add the flour mixture to the chocolate, stirring until just combined. Spread the batter evenly into the prepared pan. Sprinkle the top of the batter with the remaining 1 cup [180 g] of chocolate morsels.

6. Place the pan in the oven and bake for 25 to 30 minutes, rotating the pan about halfway through the baking time to ensure even cooking, until the brownies are set and the edges looked baked.

7. Remove the brownies from the oven and place on a wire rack to cool in the pan.

8. Cut the brownies into 6 large squares. Serve topped with vanilla ice cream and chocolate sauce, if desired.

Buttermiziilk Pound Cake Cake Cake Cake

Ain't nuthin' like a nice, round pound cake! Get your head out the gutter—I'm not talking about Shorty from the club with the big ol' backside. I'm talking about that buttermilk cake sweetness, that fluffy stuff that has you coming back for more every time. What a treat!

SERVES 6 TO 8

INGREDIENTS

1½ cups [210 g] all-purpose flour
1 tsp baking powder
½ tsp salt
10 Tbsp [150 g] unsalted butter, at room temperature
1 cup [200 g] granulated sugar
2 large eggs
1 large egg yolk
1½ tsp pure vanilla extract
⅔ cup [160 ml] buttermilk
Whipped cream and fresh berries, for serving

1. Preheat the oven to 350°F [180°C], with a rack in the middle position. Coat a 9-by-5-by-3-in [23-by-12-by-7.5-cm] loaf pan with nonstick cooking spray or softened butter. Line the bottom and the two short ends of the pan with parchment paper, letting the paper extend over the top edges of the pan, and coat again with the spray or butter. Dust the pan with flour, knocking out any excess, and set aside.

2. In a medium bowl, whisk the flour, baking powder, and salt. Set aside.

3. In the bowl of a stand mixer fitted with the paddle attachment, or in a large bowl and using a handheld electric mixer, cream together the butter and granulated sugar on medium-high speed until light and fluffy, at least 5 minutes, scraping down the bowl with a rubber spatula, as needed.

4. With the mixer running on medium speed, one at a time, add the eggs and egg yolk, beating for 1 minute after each addition. Scrape down the bowl with a rubber spatula, add the vanilla, and beat until just incorporated.

5. With the mixer running on low speed, add the dry ingredients in three additions, alternating with the buttermilk, beginning and ending with the dry ingredients. Scrape down the bowl with a rubber spatula, as needed. Stop the mixer when a few streaks of flour remain and finish mixing by hand until the ingredients are incorporated. Transfer the batter to the prepared pan, smoothing the top.

6. Place the loaf pan in the oven and bake for 55 to 60 minutes, rotating the pan halfway through the baking time to ensure even cooking. The pound cake is done when a toothpick inserted into the center of the cake comes out with a moist crumb or two attached. Remove the pan from the oven and let sit for 10 to 15 minutes, or until the pan is cool enough to handle. Remove the pound cake from the pan, place it on a wire rack, and let cool completely.

7. Serve with a dollop of lightly sweetened whipped cream and a handful of fresh berries..

THA FLIP

Ain't nuthin' basic about this base, but you can also make it sing with some raspberry. Purée 1½ [180 g] cups fresh raspberries in a food processor or blender with ¼ cup [50 g] granulated sugar. Transfer half the pound cake batter to the prepared pan. Spread half the raspberry purée on top. Top the purée with the remaining half of the batter and spread with the other half of the purée. Using a long wooden skewer, make swirls in the cake with the purée, inserting the skewer all the way to the bottom of the cake so both layers of purée are swirled. So neat and so sweet.

DESSERT

Rags to Riches Apple Pie

What's more American than the good ol' rags to riches story of the Big Snoopy D-O-Double G? Yours truly, that is. Well, maybe some good old classic apple pie. When you serve it up to your crew, make sure to share a story about me.

SERVES 8

FOR THE PIECRUST:
- 2½ cups [350 g] all-purpose flour, plus more for the work surface
- 2 Tbsp granulated sugar
- ½ tsp baking powder
- 1 tsp salt
- 8 Tbsp [1 stick, or 110 g] unsalted butter, chilled
- ½ cup [90 g] vegetable shortening, chilled

FOR THE FILLING:
- 2 lb [910 g] Granny Smith apples, about 10 medium apples
- ¼ cup [60 ml] freshly squeezed lemon juice
- 6 Tbsp [80 g] granulated sugar
- 2 Tbsp cornstarch
- 1½ tsp ground cinnamon
- ¼ tsp salt
- 3 Tbsp unsalted butter, cubed

FOR THE EGG WASH:
- 1 large egg
- ¼ tsp salt

Turbinado sugar, for sprinkling (optional)

TO MAKE THE PIECRUST:

1. In a food processor, combine the flour, sugar, baking powder, and salt. Process briefly to combine.

2. Cut the butter and shortening into cubes and add to the food processor. Pulse until the mixture resembles coarse meal. Dump the mixture into a large bowl.

3. A little at a time, add about 6 Tbsp [90 ml] of water (you may not need it all)

CONTINUED

and mix with a wooden spoon, or your hands, until a bit of dough can be pinched together between two fingers and hold its shape. Using your hands, knead the dough in the bowl as best you can to incorporate all the crumbly bits. Divide the dough in half, wrap each piece in plastic wrap, and refrigerate for at least 2 hours, or preferably overnight.

TO MAKE THE FILLING:

1. Peel the apples and slice them into ¼-in [6-mm] wedges. Slice the wedges in half widthwise and place them in a large bowl. Add the lemon juice, tossing to coat.

2. Add the sugar, cornstarch, cinnamon, and salt. Using your hands or a wooden spoon, toss the ingredients until combined. Set aside.

TO FINISH THE PIECRUST AND ASSEMBLE THE PIE:

1. Place one dough ball on a lightly floured work surface. Roll the dough into a large circle, slightly larger than the bottom of a 9-in [23-cm] pie plate. Transfer the crust to the plate and gently press it in.

2. Add the apple filling to the crust. Dot the top of the filling with the butter cubes.

3. Roll out the remaining piece of dough into a slightly larger circle than the first. Place it over the filling. Decoratively crimp the edges. Make two slits in the top crust to allow the pie to vent while baking.

TO MAKE THE EGG WASH:

1. In a small bowl, whisk the egg and salt until well combined. Brush the top piecrust with the egg wash.

2. Sprinkle the top crust with the turbinado sugar and freeze the pie for 1 hour.

TO FINISH THE PIE:

1. Preheat the oven to 425°F [220°C], with a rack in the middle position.

2. Remove the pie from the freezer and place it on a baking sheet. Place the sheet in the oven and bake the pie for 50 to 60 minutes, rotating halfway through the baking time to ensure even cooking. The pie is done when the top is nicely browned and the filling is bubbling through the vents. Tent the pie with aluminum foil if the crust browns before the filling bubbles.

3. Remove the pie from the oven and let rest for at least 1 hour, or longer, to let the juices and filling settle.

4. Serve with vanilla ice cream, if desired. The pie will keep on the counter, lightly covered in plastic wrap, for up to 3 days.

Gimme S'mores Pie

I was never much of a boy scout—tying knots, sewing badges—all that shit was never for the young Dogg. The only part I could really get on board with is lightin' up those s'mores over the campfire—although I'd rather be lightin' up something else. This s'mores pie recipe takes those campfire-side treats and gives them an upgrade courtesy of a graham cracker cr-izz-ust. Whether you're a weenie boy scout or a bad boy like Bigg Snoop, everyone will agree this pie is fire.

SERVES 8

FOR THE GRAHAM CRACKER CRUST:

- 1½ cups [180 g] graham cracker crumbs, from 10 to 12 whole crackers, plus more crumbs for garnishing (optional)
- 3 Tbsp packed light brown sugar
- ¼ tsp salt
- 6 Tbsp [85 g] unsalted butter, melted

FOR THE CHOCOLATE FILLING:

- 1 cup [200 g] granulated sugar
- ½ cup [40 g] cocoa powder
- ¼ cup [35 g] cornstarch
- ¾ tsp salt
- 2 cups [480 ml] whole milk
- 1¼ cups [300 ml] heavy cream
- 1 large egg, lightly beaten
- 1 Tbsp pure vanilla extract

FOR THE MARSHMALLOW TOPPING:

- 3 large egg whites
- 1¼ cups [250 g] granulated sugar
- ½ tsp cream of tartar
- ¼ tsp salt
- 1 Tbsp pure vanilla extract

TO MAKE THE GRAHAM CRACKER CRUST:

In a medium bowl, combine the graham cracker crumbs, brown sugar, and salt. Whisk to combine. Add the melted butter. Using a rubber spatula, mix until the crumbs are moistened. Transfer the crumbs to a 9-in [23-cm] pie plate and firmly press them into the bottom and up the sides. After pressing with your fingers, use a measuring cup or straight-sided glass to tightly secure the crumbs into place. Freeze the crust for at least 1 hour, and up to overnight.

TO MAKE THE CHOCOLATE FILLING:

1. In a medium saucepan, whisk the sugar, cocoa powder, cornstarch, and salt. Add the milk and cream and whisk again to blend.

2. Add the egg and place the saucepan over medium-high heat. Whisking constantly, cook until the mixture begins to thicken and bubbles begin popping on the surface. Decrease the heat to medium and whisk vigorously for 45 seconds. Remove the pan from the heat.

3. Strain the filling through a fine-mesh sieve into a heat-proof bowl. Add the vanilla and whisk until incorporated. Place a piece of plastic wrap directly onto the pudding's surface. Refrigerate until chilled, 2 to 4 hours, stirring occasionally.

4. Once cool, add the filling to the piecrust and place the pie in the refrigerator.

TO MAKE THE MARSH-MALLOW TOPPING:

1. Place the bowl of a stand mixer, or other heat-proof bowl, over a pot of simmering water. Do not let the bottom of the bowl touch the water. Add the egg whites, sugar, cream of tartar, salt, and ¼ cup [60 ml] of water. Cook, whisking, until warm to the touch, 3 to 4 minutes.

2. Remove the bowl from the hot water and attach it to your stand mixer fitted with the whisk attachment. Alternatively, use a hand-held electric mixer. Whisk on medium-high to high speed for 7 minutes.

3. Add the vanilla. Continue whisking for 2 minutes more until thick and glossy.

4. Remove the pie from the refrigerator. Working quickly, as the topping begins to set as it cools, spread the warm marshmallow over the top—there will be lots of marshmallow.

5. Toast the marshmallow with a mini kitchen torch. Alternatively, preheat the broiler, with a rack in the top third of the oven. Place the pie briefly under the broiler, watching it closely so it doesn't burn.

6. Slice and serve immediately sprinkled with graham cracker crumbs (if using), or refrigerate for up to 2 hours. The pie is best the day it is made, but will keep, refrigerated and lightly covered in plastic wrap, for 1 to 2 days.

THA FLIP

If you don't have time to make the graham cracker crust, it's still hot with a store-bought pie crust.

DIPPED

and

WHIPPED STRAW-BERRIES

MAKES ABOUT 20 CHOCOLATE-COVERED STRAW-BERRIES

Sometimes the **BIGG DOGG** and his **BOSS LADY** gotta get real sensual on date night—light some scented candles, break out the rose petals, and dine on a couple of these chocolate-dipped strawberries. For maximum effect, I gotta get my *Coming to America* on and have my baby boo feed 'em to me in the tub. **REAL PLAYA**, you know what I'm talkin' about?

1   lb [455 g] fresh strawberries (do not remove the stems) washed and air-dried completely

1½ cups [270 g] semisweet chocolate chips
½   cup [90 g] white chocolate chips

1. Line a baking sheet with parchment paper or wax paper and set aside.

2. Make a double boiler: Suspend a small heat-proof bowl over a small pot of simmering water set over medium heat. Do not let the bottom of the bowl touch the water. Add the semisweet chocolate chips to melt, stirring occasionally with a rubber spatula until smooth. Alternatively, place the semisweet chips in a microwave-safe bowl and microwave on high power in 30-second bursts, stirring after each, until the chocolate is melted and smooth. Once melted, remove the bowl from the heat/microwave.

3. Holding a strawberry by its stem, blot it dry with a paper towel. Dip it into the melted chocolate, allowing the excess to drip back into the bowl before carefully placing the strawberry on the prepared baking sheet. If the stem comes off while dipping, use a fork to remove the strawberry from the chocolate. If the chocolate cools while you are working, place it back on the stovetop, or in the microwave, and reheat.

4. Repeat with the remaining strawberries. Let the chocolate set before moving onto the next step. You can speed this up by placing the sheet in the refrigerator or freezer.

5. Using the double boiler again, place the white chocolate in a clean small heat-proof bowl suspended over the same pot of simmering water. Do not let the bottom of the bowl touch the water. Stir with a clean rubber spatula until melted. Alternatively, follow the directions in step 2 for melting in the microwave.

6. Carefully transfer the melted white chocolate to a ziplock bag. Seal the bag and snip a tiny hole from one lower corner of the bag. Pipe the white chocolate decoratively over the strawberries. Refrigerate the decorated strawberries for at least 30 minutes to set. The strawberries will keep, refrigerated and lightly covered in plastic wrap, for up to 3 days.

Go Shorty, It's Your Birthday Cake

Birthdays are the best. Everybody treating you like royalty, and you get all the goodies that come with it—I'm talking birthday cards, birthday presents, and, oh yeah, that birthday cake. This recipe will have you celebrating after every mouthful. And after you finished that last slice, there's only one thing left—breaking out your birthday suit for some of that birthday sex. Shout-out to my man Jeremih!

SERVES 10 TO 12

FOR THE CHOCOLATE CAKE:

2   cups [280 g] all-purpose flour
2   cups [400 g] granulated sugar
¾   cup [60 g] cocoa powder
2   tsp baking powder
1½ tsp baking soda
½   tsp salt
1   cup [240 ml] buttermilk
½   cup [120 ml] vegetable oil
3   large eggs
2   tsp pure vanilla extract
1   cup [240 ml] boiling water

FOR THE CHOCOLATE FROSTING:

24 Tbsp [3 sticks, or 330 g] unsalted butter, at room temperature
1   cup [80 g] cocoa powder
5   cups [600 g] confectioners' sugar
½   cup [120 ml] whole milk, plus more as needed
1   tsp pure vanilla extract

    Chocolate sprinkles, for garnishing

TO MAKE THE CHOCO-LATE CAKE:

1. Preheat the oven to 350°F [180°C], with a rack in the middle position. Butter two 9-in [23-cm] round cake pans. Lightly dust the pans with flour and knock out any excess. Set aside.

2. In the bowl of a stand mixer fitted with the paddle attachment, or in a large bowl and using a handheld electric mixer, combine the flour, granulated sugar, cocoa powder, baking powder, baking soda, and salt. Whisk to combine.

3. Add the buttermilk, vegetable oil, eggs, and vanilla. Mix on medium speed until combined. Reduce the speed to low and, with the mixer running, carefully add the boiling water to the batter. Continue mixing until everything is combined. Evenly divide the batter between the prepared pans.

4. Put the pans in the oven and bake for 30 to 35 minutes, rotating the pans halfway through the baking time to ensure even cooking, or until a toothpick inserted into the center of the cake comes out clean.

TO MAKE THE CHOCO-LATE FROSTING:

1. While the cake bakes, in a large bowl and using a handheld electric mixer, cream the butter and cocoa powder until blended and smooth.

2. Add the confectioners' sugar, milk, and vanilla. Beat on high speed for about 1 minute. If the frosting is too dry add a bit more milk, a little at a time, until the right consistency is achieved. Cover and refrigerate the frosting until needed; bring to room temperature before using.

TO ASSEMBLE THE BIRTHDAY CAKE:

1. Remove the cakes from the oven and place on a wire rack to cool for 10 minutes. Run a knife around the inside edges of the pans to loosen the layers. Turn the layers out of the pans onto the rack to cool completely.

2. Place the bottom layer on a cake plate or cake stand, flat-side down. Using an offset spatula, spread about one-third of the frosting on top of the layer, all the way to the edges.

3. Carefully position the second layer on top of the first, flat-side down, pressing slightly to adhere the two layers. Spread another third of the frosting over the top, spreading it all the way to the edges. Frost the sides of the cake with the remaining frosting, turning the plate or stand as you work.

4. Decorate the cake with sprinkles on top, or all over, as you like it.

Hustle Hard Chocolate Cheesecake

Back in the day, my man Puff Daddy would send his people all around New York City to find him that perfect cheesecake. You ain't gonna find the latest and greatest in the tri-state area though. My cheesecake is bomb enough to make Puff hop that private jet from the Big Apple to the LBC. Now that I'm sharing this recipe, the best dessert ain't an East Coast thang or a West Coast thang. It's a worldwide thang, and it's coming straight to your kitchen.

SERVES 10 TO 12

FOR THE CHOCOLATE CRUST:

9 oz [255 g] chocolate wafer cookies, about 45 two-in [5-cm] thin wafer cookies
3 Tbsp granulated sugar
½ tsp salt
8 Tbsp [1 stick, or 110 g] unsalted butter, melted

FOR THE CHOCOLATE FILLING:

1½ cups [270 g] dark chocolate chips
24 oz [680 g] cream cheese, at room temperature
1¼ cups [150 g] confectioners' sugar
¾ tsp salt
5 Tbsp [75 g] sour cream
1 tsp pure vanilla extract

Cocoa powder, for dusting

TO MAKE THE CHOCOLATE CRUST:

1. Coat a 9-in [23-cm] springform pan with cooking spray or softened butter. Line the bottom and sides with parchment paper and set aside.

2. In a food processer, combine the chocolate wafers, sugar, and salt. Process until finely ground. Add the melted butter. Pro-

cess until the crumbs are uniformly moistened, scraping down the bowl, if necessary. Alternatively, place the wafers, sugar, and salt in a large ziplock bag, seal the bag, pressing out as much air as possible, and smash with a rolling pin. Transfer the crumbs to a medium bowl and add the melted butter. Using a rubber spatula, stir to combine.

3. Transfer the buttered crumbs to the prepared pan and firmly press them into the bottom and halfway up the sides of the pan. After pressing with your fingers, use a measuring cup or straight-sided glass to tightly secure the crumbs into place. Freeze the crust for at least 1 hour, and up to overnight.

TO MAKE THE CHOCOLATE FILLING:

1. Place a medium heat-proof bowl over a pot of simmering water. Do not let the bottom of the bowl touch the water. Add the chocolate chips to melt, stirring with a rubber spatula occasionally until melted and smooth. Alter-

natively, place the chocolate chips in a medium microwave-safe bowl and microwave on high power in 30-second bursts, stirring after each, until the chocolate is melted and smooth. Let cool to room temperature before using.

2. In the bowl of a stand mixer fitted with the paddle attachment, or in a large bowl and using a handheld electric mixer, combine the cream cheese, confectioners' sugar, and salt. Beat on medium-low speed until smooth, scraping the bowl with a rubber spatula, as needed.

3. Add the sour cream to the cooled chocolate and whisk to blend. Add the chocolate mixture to the cream cheese mixture. Beat on medium-low speed until smooth. Add the vanilla and beat for 30 seconds more. Transfer the filling to the prepared crust, smoothing the top with an offset spatula or butter knife. Cover the cake with plastic wrap and refrigerate for 4 to 5 hours to set.

4. When ready to serve, carefully remove the sides of the pan. To remove the bottom, slide a long serrated knife between the crust and the metal bottom to loosen. Place the cake on a serving plate. Using a serrated knife, slice the cake into wedges. Run the knife under hot water each time you make a cut to ensure clean slices. Serve the slices with a dusting of cocoa powder.

5. The cake will keep, refrigerated and tightly wrapped in plastic wrap, for up to 3 days, but is best the day it is made.

OG MUNCHIES
*
CANDY ROUNDUP

~ 1 ~
STARBURSTS

Real chewy, real fruity, and real good. Yeah, I got a strain to go with every flavor. I'm like the sommelier of Starbursts. I'll hit you that right mix. Just keep those lemons to yourself though—we all know the reds and pinks lead the pack.

~ 2 ~
SKITTLES

One of my go-to candies when I get those late-night munchies are Skittles. I make sure to always keep a jumbo bag ready for myself— and for those that pop up backstage after the show to visit Tha Dogg in his element.

~ 3 ~
BABY RUTH MINIS

A smoker's delight. I keep the minis around so you all don't get too greedy. This ain't Halloween and I damn sure ain't tricking. The flavor of those chewy minis is definitely a treat though, and you do know that.

~ 4 ~
ORBITZ

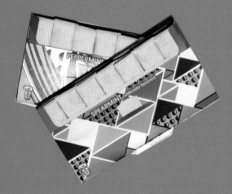

When you spit fresh like I do, you always gotta keep your breath on point. What I look like going into the booth with some musty breath coming outta my grill? That's why Orbitz always keep the Boss Dogg ice cool.

~ 5 ~
TWIZZLERS/ RED VINES

Ain't nuthin' like taking it all the way back to your childhood and chewing on one of these. And it's still funny to take one and slap the homie on the back of his neck when he ain't looking!

CHAPTER 5

Drinks

OG Gin and Juice [133]

Remix Gin and Juice [136] That Goody Gimlet [138]

Jet Settin' Negroni [139] So Clean We Dirty Martini [141] Wake 'n' Bake Corpse Reviver [142]

Happy Hour Vodka Cranberry [143] French Connect 75 [144] That Thang Singapore Sling [146]

EVERYONE KNOWS THAT my drink of choice is gin and juice. I've been reppin' Tanqueray since I dropped my first album *Doggystyle* in '93, and I'm still rockin' with it to this day. Take a guess who holds the Guinness world record for the world's biggest gin and juice? That's right—Tha Bigg Boss Dogg. Man, I even put a twist on the recipe with the Tanqueray "Laid Back" cocktail—that gin tastes real good when it's mixed with a splash of pineapple and some of my man Puff's Cîroc. Ooh-wee!

Ever since I teamed up with my homegirl Martha, she's been introducing me to a lot of other cocktails—fancy scotches and rums and all kinds of drinks that will have you feeling real buzzed. Sampling all those crazy alcohols has made me a real liquor connoisseur. Ya dig? I've been experimenting with a few of 'em, so here's some recipes for the next time you and the crew are trying to function.

OG Gin and Juice

Rollin' down the street, smokin' endo…yeah, you know the rest. It's been my drink of choice since the homies were swiping bottles from the liquor store. If you wanted to sip with me back then, you had to kick in a few bucks. Everybody had their cups but if they ain't chipped in, the young Snoop Doggy Dogg wasn't having it. But, if you had a couple bills, I would maybe share my concoction with ya.

INGREDIENTS
Gin
Orange Juice

Take some gin, take some juice, mix it up. That's it.

06
Gin and Juice

Remix Gin and Juice

After the original comes the remix. After 25 years of mixing that Tanqueray with the OJ, it was time to put a fresh twist on the classic. And boy, did I do it with the Tanqueray "Laid Back!" We still add a splash of juice, only now we hit it with that pineapple to give the whole thang a tropical vibe. To get extra lit, we top it all off with some of that Cîroc vodka. Bingo—Gin and Juice 2.0.

SERVES 1

INGREDIENTS
1   oz [30 ml] gin (Tanqueray, preferably)
1   oz [30 ml] apple-flavored vodka
2   oz [60 ml] pineapple juice
    Pineapple leaves and a lime wheel, for garnishing

1. Fill a cocktail shaker with ice. Add the gin, vodka, and pineapple juice. Stir.

2. Strain into a rocks glass and garnish with the pineapple leaves and lime wheel. Serve immediately.

That Goody Gimlet

For you bougie mofos, here's a cocktail that's a little more high class than the gin and juice I was swiggin' from a plastic cup. It's even got a fancy-ass name: the Gimlet.

SERVES 1

INGREDIENTS

2   oz [60 ml] gin (Tanqueray, preferably)
1   oz [30 ml] freshly squeezed lime juice
½   oz [15 ml] Simplest Syrup (page 144)
     Club soda, for topping
     Lime wheel, for garnishing

1. Chill a coupe glass.

2. Fill a cocktail shaker with ice. Add the gin, lime juice, and simple syrup. Cover the shaker and shake well for 30 seconds.

3. Strain into the chilled coupe glass and top with club soda. Garnish with the lime wheel and serve immediately.

Jet Settin' Negroni

Nah, it ain't no Peroni; it's a Negroni. This Italian cocktail will leave you feeling so good, you'll swear you're fly enough to be a Milan fashion model or somethin'. Yeah, that vermouth in the mix will have you feeling real silky smooth. Just know your limits, 'cause too many of these will have you going from runway ready to certified sloppy!

SERVES 1

INGREDIENTS

1   oz [30 ml] gin (Tanqueray, preferably)
1   oz [30 ml] Campari
1   oz [30 ml] sweet vermouth
    Orange peel, for garnishing

1. Fill a cocktail shaker with ice. Add the gin, Campari, and sweet vermouth. Stir.

2. Fill a rocks glass with ice. Strain the Negroni into the glass. Add the orange peel and serve immediately.

So Clean We Dirty Martini

Take note, Gs—clean-cut ain't always gonna cut it. Your girl likes a dirty Dogg, and I'll have her feelin' right with this dirty martini. Shaken not stirred like my man James Bond might say. And what do me and Bond have in common? We're both a couple of players with great taste in cocktails. How 'bout that?

SERVES 1

INGREDIENTS

3   oz [90 ml] gin (Tanqueray, preferably)
1   oz [30 ml] dry vermouth
    Splash of olive brine
3   pimiento-stuffed Spanish olives

1. Chill a martini glass.

2. Fill a cocktail shaker with ice. Add the gin, vermouth, and olive brine. Cover the shaker and shake well for 30 seconds.

3. Strain into the chilled martini glass. Add the olives and serve immediately.

Wake 'n' Bake Corpse Reviver

Got that nasty hangover from dropping it like it's hot at the club a li'l too long last night? Well then, Tha Dogg's got this hair of the dogg to get you back up and at 'em. The money ain't sitting around waiting; you need to get up, get out, and get something.

SERVES 1

INGREDIENTS

1   oz [30 ml] gin (Tanqueray, preferably)
1   oz [30 ml] Cointreau
1   oz [30 ml] sweet vermouth
¼   oz [7 ml] freshly squeezed lemon juice
    Orange peel, for garnishing

1. Chill a martini glass

2. Fill a cocktail shaker with ice. Add the gin, Cointreau, vermouth, and lemon juice. Cover the shaker and shake well for 30 seconds.

3. Strain into the chilled martini glass and garnish with the orange peel. Serve immediately.

Happy Hour Vodka Cranberry

This one is a simple classic. When you want that clean refresher, drop a little cranberry in that Cîroc. It's happy hour. Don't meet me there—beat me there!

SERVES 1

INGREDIENTS

1   oz [30 ml] vodka
1   oz [30 ml] cranberry juice
¼   oz [7.5 ml] freshly squeezed lime
     juice
     Lime wheel, for garnishing

1. Chill a rocks glass.

2. Fill a cocktail shaker with ice.

3. Add the vodka, cranberry juice, and lime juice. Cover the shaker and shake well for 30 seconds.

4. Strain into the chilled rocks glass and garnish with a lime wheel. Serve immediately.

French Connect 75

This cocktail is something I can rock with—that champagne adds some extra pizzazz to the gin. Add some simple syrup to keep things sweet and you got a *tres bon* drink. *Oui, oui*!

SERVES 1

INGREDIENTS

2 oz [60 ml] gin (Tanqueray, preferably)

½ oz [15 ml] freshly squeezed lemon juice

½ oz [15 ml] Simplest Syrup (see left)

2 oz [60 ml] Champagne

Lemon twist, for garnishing

1. Chill a Champagne flute.

2. Fill a cocktail shaker with ice. Add the gin, lemon juice, and simple syrup. Cover the shaker and shake well for 30 seconds.

3. Strain into the chilled Champagne flute and top with the Champagne. Garnish with the lemon twist and serve immediately.

SIMPLEST SYRUP

Making simple syrup is the easiest way to up your cocktail game. In a saucepan over medium heat, boil 2 cups [480 ml] of water and 2 cups [400 g] of granulated sugar. Stir real fast until the sugar dissolves. Let that baby cool to room temp and store it in a sealed container for up to 1 month in the fridge. Break it out whenever it's time to party.

That Thang Singapore Sling

The city, the country, the island. It's all Singapore. One of the few places on God's green earth that Tha Dogg has yet to roam. I'ma scratch it off my bucket list one day. But in the meantime, in-between time, why don't you and me take a trip to the corner store and we'll get this thang crackin' right now.

SERVES 1

INGREDIENTS

3   oz [90 ml] pineapple juice
1   oz [30 ml] gin (Tanqueray, preferably)
½   oz [15 ml] Cointreau
¼   oz [7 ml] freshly squeezed lime juice
¼   oz [7 ml] grenadine
   Club soda, for topping

1. Chill a Collins glass

2. Fill a cocktail shaker with ice. Add the pineapple juice, gin, Cointreau, lime juice, and grenadine. Cover the shaker and shake well for 30 seconds.

3. Strain into the chilled Collins glass and top with club soda. Serve immediately.

CHAPTER 6

Parties

Thanksgiving: At My House [150]
Game Day: Time for Football [162]
Game Night: All About the Dominoes [172]
From Tha Beach: Seafood Remix [178]

Thanksgiving: At My House

YOU BETTER BELIEVE IT—Thanksgiving is one of the most important cooking days of the year. It's real important that you have a great chef in the kitchen on T-Day. I'm talking about your momma, your auntie...someone who knows just how much cheese to put in that macaroni, or who makes the perfect gravy to cover your whole plate. I just so happen to have learned all the greatest Broadus family recipes from my grandmas, cousins, you name it. Some of these recipes weren't easy to come by—you know the family ain't trying to give up their secrets! Well, I struggled to get 'em so you don't have to. Your turkey will never be dry and your sides will never be flavorless if you follow Tha Dogg's lead!

Ain't No Jive Herbed Turkey and Gravy 154

Good Good Green Beans 158   M.O.P.:

Mash Out

Potatoes 159   My My

My Sweet Potato

Pie 160   Rags to

Riches Apple Pie 115

BEATS
and
BITES

We giving thanks during T-Day, so it's only right we pick songs that represent that. The Clark Sisters will have everyone saying "HALLELUJAH" before you take that first bite. Your aunties and your grandma will be up dancing by the time Stevie comes on, and we close things out with my man Busta. On a day like this, there's no more appropriate message than "THANK YOU."

~ 1 ~
BLESSED & HIGHLY FAVORED
THE CLARK SISTERS

~ 2 ~
LOVE ON TOP
BEYONCÉ

~ 3 ~
THE JOY
JAY-Z & KANYE WEST

~ 4 ~
KEEP YA HEAD UP
2PAC

~ 5 ~
BEFORE I LET GO
MAZE

~ 6 ~
EXTREMELY BLESSED
2 CHAINZ

~ 7 ~
DO I DO
STEVIE WONDER

~ 8 ~
BLACK OR WHITE
MICHAEL JACKSON

~ 9 ~
I'M COMING OUT
DIANA ROSS

~ 10 ~
THANK YOU
BUSTA RHYMES

Ain't No Jive Herbed Turkey and Gravy

What's Thanksgiving without the big bird? If you're lucky enough to find a seat at the table, you get to chow on my turkey that's heavy on the orange zest and orange gravy. Yeah, most use lemon, but I'm a leader, not a follower. The results speak for themselves and you ain't ever going back to lemon after you try this.

SERVES 8 TO 12

FOR THE HERBED TURKEY:

1   12- to 14-lb [4.6- to 6.4-kg] whole turkey, thawed if frozen

¼   cup [40 g] kosher salt, plus more for seasoning

2   medium oranges

1   1½-oz [40-g] package fresh "poultry herbs," or 2 sprigs sage, 8 sprigs thyme, and 2 sprigs rosemary), plus more for decorating

8   Tbsp [1 stick, or 110 g] unsalted butter, at room temperature

3   garlic cloves, minced
    Cracked black pepper

3   medium yellow onions, each cut into 8 wedges

FOR THE GRAVY:

1¼ cups [300 ml] chicken stock or broth

2   Tbsp all-purpose flour

4   sprigs flat-leaf parsley, stems removed and leaves finely chopped (optional)

TO MAKE THE HERBED TURKEY:

1. The night before you plan to cook the turkey, remove the packaging and giblet bag from the cavity. Working in your clean kitchen sink, rinse the outside and inside of the turkey and pat it dry with paper towels. Sprinkle the salt onto the turkey and use your hands to rub it evenly all over the skin. Transfer the turkey to a rimmed baking sheet and refrigerate, uncovered, overnight, or up to 24 hours.

2. The day you plan to cook the turkey, make the herb butter: Using a rasp-style grater, remove the zest from 1 orange and put the zest into a medium bowl; reserve the zested orange. Pick the leaves from the sprigs of sage, thyme, and rosemary and finely chop them together; reserve all the stems. Add the chopped herbs to the orange zest. Add the butter and garlic. Stir until everything is evenly combined.

3. Preheat the oven to 325°F [165°C], with a rack in the lower third of the oven.

4. Remove the turkey on the baking sheet from the refrigerator and transfer the turkey to the clean kitchen sink; reserve the baking sheet. Rinse the turkey and pat it dry with paper towels. Insert your fingers between the skin and meat over the breasts and thighs to separate the skin from the meat, taking care not to tear it or remove it from the turkey. Using a spoon, gently lift the skin and place spoonfuls of the herb butter between the skin and meat all over the turkey. Use your hands to press and spread the butter evenly. Rub any herb butter left in the bowl all over the outside of the turkey. Liberally season the turkey with pepper.

5. Place 8 onion wedges into the cavity of the turkey and add the reserved herb stems. Group the remaining onion wedges in the center of the rimmed baking sheet so they touch. Center the turkey on top of the onions. Place the turkey in the oven. Bake for 2 to 2½ hours until golden brown on the outside and an instant-read thermometer inserted into the thigh (not touching the bone) reads at least 165°F [75°C].

6. Remove the turkey from the oven and let rest for 20 minutes. Using a meat fork or wooden spoon inserted into the turkey's cavity, gently lift it off the baking sheet and onto a large cutting board. Tent the turkey loosely with aluminum foil.

TO MAKE THE GRAVY:

1. Set a strainer over a glass measuring cup and pour the sheet pan drippings and onions into it. While the drippings drain, squeeze the juice from both oranges. Once the drippings have fully drained, set the onions aside in a small bowl. Spoon off 2 Tbsp of the fat that rises to the surface of the drippings and place in a medium saucepan; continue removing the remaining fat; discard it or save for another use. Once all the fat is removed, add the orange juice to the drippings. Add enough chicken stock to make 2 cups [480 ml] of liquid.

CONTINUED

2. Place the saucepan over medium-high heat to warm the rendered fat. Add half the drained onions (reserve the other half). Cook for 3 to 5 minutes, stirring, until the onions start to fall apart and caramelize at the edges.

3. Add the flour. Cook for 1 minute, stirring constantly. Stir in the drippings-and-juice mixture and bring to a simmer. Adjust the heat to medium-low to maintain a gentle simmer. Cook for 6 to 8 minutes, stirring occasionally, until reduced to a thick gravy. Remove the pan from the heat and season with salt and pepper. If you like a smooth gravy, transfer it to a blender and purée until smooth, or leave as is with pieces of onion. Stir in the parsley (if using) and pour the gravy into a serving bowl or gravy boat.

TO SERVE, FOLLOW THE GREAT 8

Let me run this thing down for ya real simple like:

1. Snip those legs away, both legs, separating the thighs from the drumsticks.
2. Remove the bones from the thighs and roughly chop the thigh meat.
3. Cut away the breasts in whole pieces then cut crosswise into slices to your liking.
4. Remove the wings as whole pieces.
5. Arrange the breast slices together in the center of a serving platter.
6. Place the wings together on one side and the drumsticks together on the opposite side.
7. Pile the thigh meat below the breast slices and pile the reserved roasted onion wedges above it.
8. Garnish the platter with fresh herb sprigs and serve warm with the gravy.

Good Good Green Beans

Now, you ain't getting the most colorful palettes represented on your plate on Thanksgiving. There's a whole lot of grays and oranges. But if you know Big Snoop Dogg, you know I gotta have that green. We call them string beans in the hood, and this is a must have to make sure your meal is complete. Just add butter and lemon and those greens will taste as good as they look. After the meal, you can go ahead and break out those OTHER greens. Yeah, the ones that smoke as good as they smell...

SERVES 8

INGREDIENTS

	Salt
2	lb [910 g] green beans, trimmed
6	Tbsp [85 g] unsalted butter
	Zest of 1 lemon
	Cracked black pepper

1. Bring a large pot of heavily salted water to a boil over high heat. Add the green beans. Cook for 3 to 4 minutes; the beans should still be crunchy. Drain and set aside.

2. In a large skillet over medium-high heat, melt the butter. Swirl the skillet to cover the bottom completely, watching it closely until the butter browns. The butter should foam and subside, and start to smell nutty after about 5 minutes.

3. Once the skillet is hot and the foam has subsided, add the green beans. Stir to evenly coat with the browned butter.

4. Sprinkle on the lemon zest and season with salt and pepper. Sauté for 3 to 4 minutes more. Taste and add more salt and pepper, as needed.

5. The green beans can be kept covered, tented with aluminum foil, or in an oven on low heat until ready to serve.

M.O.P.: Mash Out Potatoes

This is where you load up that plate and make sure you're getting ready for the coming cold season. Even in Cali, in November, the weather starts to dip, so no need to keep that beach bod. Just as well, 'cause you know I add that cream to give my mash that classic, buttery texture. It's the holidays—relax your mind and let your conscious be free. Like Rick James says, "It's a celebration, bitches!"

SERVES 8

INGREDIENTS

Salt

4 lb [1.8 kg] Russet or Yukon gold potatoes, peeled and quartered

4 Tbsp [55 g] unsalted butter

2½ cups [600 ml] heavy cream

½ cup [120 g] mayonnaise

Cracked black pepper

1. Bring a large pot of heavily salted water to a boil over high heat. Lower the heat to medium-high and add the potatoes. Cook for 20 to 25 minutes until tender, testing with a fork. Drain and set aside, covered with a damp towel.

2. Return the pot to medium heat and add the butter to melt.

3. Add the cream and mayonnaise. Whisk until combined.

4. Return the potatoes to the pot. Using a potato masher, mash to combine the ingredients. Taste and season with salt and pepper. Serve immediately.

My My My Sweet Potato Pie

These days it's like everyone is into pumpkin spice. But you know how we do it—you can skip me with all that pumpkin nonsense. This is a real hood staple. Like my main guy Domino would say, "My my my, can I get a piece of that sweet potato pie?"

SERVES 8

FOR THE PIECRUST:

1¼	cups [175 g] all-purpose flour, plus more for the work surface
1	Tbsp granulated sugar
¼	tsp baking powder
1	tsp salt
4	Tbsp [55 g] unsalted butter, chilled
¼	cup [90 g] vegetable shortening, chilled

FOR THE FILLING:

4	large sweet potatoes, scrubbed
½	cup [120 ml] whole milk
5	Tbsp [75 ml] melted unsalted butter
2	large eggs
1	cup [200g] packed light brown sugar
1	tsp salt
½	tsp ground nutmeg
	Zest of 1 orange

TO MAKE THE PIECRUST:

1. In a food processor, combine the flour, sugar, baking powder, and salt. Process briefly to combine.

2. Cut the butter and shortening into cubes and add to the food processor. Pulse until the mixture resembles coarse meal. Dump the mixture into a large bowl.

3. A little at a time, add about 3 Tbsp [45 ml] of water—

you may not need it all—and mix with a wooden spoon, or your hands, until a bit of dough can be pinched together between two fingers and hold its shape. Using your hands, knead the dough in the bowl as best you can to incorporate all the crumbly bits. Wrap the dough in plastic wrap, and refrigerate for at least 2 hours, or preferably overnight.

TO MAKE THE FILLING:

1. Preheat the oven to 400° F [200° C], with a rack in the middle position. Lightly butter a 9-in [23-cm] pie plate and set aside.

2. Arrange the sweet potatoes on a baking sheet and transfer to the oven. Bake for 40 to 90 minutes, depending their size, until completely tender. Remove from the oven and let cool until safe to handle. Peel off the skins.

3. Place the peeled sweet potatoes in a food processor. Process until smooth. (You should have about 3 cups [600 g] sweet potato purée.) Add the milk, melted butter, eggs, brown sugar, salt, nutmeg,

and orange zest. Process until smooth, stopping to scrape down the bowl, if needed. Set aside.

TO FINISH THE PIE:

1. Place the dough on a lightly floured work surface and roll into a large circle, slightly larger than the bottom of a 9-in [23-cm] pie plate. Transfer the crust to the plate and gently press it in.

2. Add the sweet potato filling to the crust.

3. Place the pie on a baking sheet and place in the oven. Bake the pie for 60 to 90 minutes, rotating halfway through the baking time to ensure even cooking. Tent the pie with aluminum foil if the crust browns before the filling is set. The pie is done when a knife inserted into the center comes out clean and the crust is golden-brown. Cool completely and serve at room temperature.

4. The pie can be kept, covered in the refrigerator for up to 3 days, or tightly wrapped in plastic wrap and aluminum foil in the freezer for up to 2 months.

Game Day: Time for Football

IT'S NO SECRET THAT Tha Bigg Boss Dogg is a die-hard Pittsburgh Steelers fan, and few events are as important to yours truly as game day. I even coach my own youth football league, the SYFL. Yeah, coaching is a blast but sometimes you just gotta sit back and be a spectator. When I'm not busy as Coach Snoop I like to chill in one of my entertainment rooms—reclined on the couch and ready to enjoy some great football. To really set things off, you know I need the perfect snacks for the Snooperbowl viewing party. Whatever team your homies are supporting, you can bet all of them are gonna agree on these championship munchies.

Squad Up Chili Cheese Fries [166]

Suited and Booted Loaded Nachos [168]

Hot Like a Skillet Pizza [170]

Gimme S'mores Pie [118]

BEATS
and
BITES

I'm competitive when it comes to game day. As far as I'm concerned, winnin' ain't everything—it's the only thing. I started this playlist with my man Khaled's anthem, "ALL I DO IS WIN." I just so happened to drop a cold verse on that one. From there, I'm keeping the energy high with those real triumphant tracks, like "WE WILL ROCK YOU." I had to close it out with the classic "EYE OF THE TIGER," although "EYE OF THA DOGG" would be a better title...

~ 1 ~
ALL I DO IS WIN
DJ KHALED

~ 2 ~
BLACK & YELLOW
WIZ KHALIFA

~ 3 ~
BEAT UP ON YO PADS
SNOOP DOGG

~ 4 ~
WELCOME TO THE JUNGLE
GUNS N ROSES

~ 5 ~
WE WILL ROCK YOU
QUEEN

~ 6 ~
LET'S GET IT STARTED
THE BLACK EYED PEAS

~ 7 ~
WHOOMP! (THERE IT IS)
TAG TEAM

~ 8 ~
MAKE 'EM SAY UHH!
MASTER P

~ 9 ~
FOREVER
DRAKE

~ 10 ~
EYE OF THE TIGER
SURVIVOR

Squad Up Chili Cheese Fries

How do you improve on french fries? Easy—by adding a whole lot of chili and cheese on top. While those fries are crinkling up in the oven, break out the ground beef and Cheddar. That chunky chili and gooey cheese takes your fries from a li'l snack to a bona fide meal. Just keep those napkins close, you hear me?

SERVES 8 TO 12

FOR THE FRIES:
4   medium Russet potatoes [about 3 lb, or 1.4 kg], peeled and cut length-wise into ½-in [12-mm] sticks
2   Tbsp vegetable oil
4   tsp smoked paprika
Salt
Cracked black pepper

FOR THE CHILI:
2   Tbsp vegetable oil
2   lb [910 g] ground beef
2   Tbsp chili powder
1   Tbsp all-purpose flour
2   tsp dried oregano
2   tsp ground cumin
1½ cups [360 ml] beef stock or broth
1   15-oz [430 g] can kidney or navy beans, drained and rinsed
Salt
Cracked black pepper

3   cups [240 g] shredded Cheddar cheese or American cheese

TO MAKE THE FRIES:

1. Preheat the oven to 425°F [220°C], with a rack in the middle position. Line a rimmed baking sheet with aluminum foil and set aside.

2. Place the potato sticks in a large bowl, cover with cold water, and drain completely; repeat twice more. Spread the potato sticks on a bed of paper towels and pat dry; dry the bowl as well. Return the potato sticks to the bowl. Add the vegetable oil and 3 tsp of

paprika. Toss to combine and coat the potatoes in the oil and spice. Spread the potato sticks evenly onto the prepared baking sheet. Season with salt and pepper.

3. Place the sheet in the oven and bake for 40 to 45 minutes, tossing and flipping the fries once halfway through the baking time to ensure even cooking, until golden brown, crisp, and tender.

TO MAKE THE CHILI:

1. While the fries bake, in a large saucepan over medium-high heat, heat the vegetable oil. Add the ground beef. Cook for about 8 minutes, stirring to break up the meat, until no longer pink. Add the chili powder, flour, oregano, and cumin. Cook for 1 minute, stirring.

2. Pour in the beef stock and add the beans. Bring the chili to a boil. Adjust the heat to medium-low to maintain a simmer, and cook for 6 to 8 minutes, stirring occasionally, until thickened. Remove the chili from the heat and season with salt and pepper.

TO FINISH:

1. When the fries are ready, remove them the oven, but leave the oven on. Spoon the chili evenly over the fries on the baking sheet. Scatter the cheese over the chili. Sprinkle the remaining 1 tsp of paprika over the cheese.

2. Return the fries to the oven. Bake for about 10 minutes until the cheese is fully melted and bubbling.

3. Remove the fries from the oven and serve immediately.

Suited and Booted Loaded Nachos

I'm all about gettin' to the bag, whether it's a bag of loot or a bag of chips. If you really wanna get your chips dipped and whipped, don't just settle for some bland sauces. My loaded nachos recipe has everything you need to take your chip game to the next level. Oh, boy!

SERVES 6 TO 8

FOR THE NACHOS:
2   Tbsp vegetable oil
1   lb [455 g] ground beef
1   tsp chili powder
1   tsp ground cumin
½   tsp garlic powder
½   tsp onion powder
2   tsp salt
2   tsp cracked black pepper
1   13-oz [370-g] bag tortilla chips

1   cup [140 g] frozen corn, thawed
1   15-oz [430-g] can black beans, drained and rinsed
1   jalepeño pepper, thinly sliced
1   cup [80 g] shredded Monterey Jack cheese
1   cup [80 g] shredded Cheddar cheese

FOR THE TOPPINGS:
2   avocados
     Juice of 1 lime
     Salt
     Cracked black pepper
¼   cup [60 g] sour cream
1   medium tomato, diced
     Fresh cilantro, for garnishing
     Sliced scallions, for garnishing

TO MAKE THE NACHOS:

1. Preheat the oven to 400°F [200°C], with a rack in the upper third position. Line a baking sheet with aluminum foil and set aside.

2. In a large skillet over medium-high, heat the vegetable oil. Swirl the skillet to cover the bottom completely. When the skillet is hot, add the ground beef, chili powder, cumin, garlic and onion powder, salt, and pepper. Cook for 6 to 7 minutes, stirring frequently to break up the meat, until the beef is completely browned. Taste and adjust for the seasonings, if necessary. Drain and discard any excess grease. Transfer the beef to a large bowl, cover, and set aside.

3. Place the tortilla chips in an even layer on the prepared baking sheet. Top the chips evenly with the ground beef. Top the beef with the corn, black beans, jalepeño, and cheeses.

4. Place the chips in the oven and bake for 6 to 7 minutes until the cheeses are completely melted.

TO FINISH THE NACHOS:

1. Meanwhile, in a small bowl, mash the avocados with the lime juice. Taste and season with salt and pepper, as needed.

2. Remove the chips from the oven and top with the mashed avocado, sour cream, and tomato. Sprinkle on the cilantro and scallions. Serve warm.

Hot Like A Skillet Pizza

When I make pizza, I mixed it up, mayne. I may put a little bit of Italian sausage, little bit of pepperoni, mozzarella, Cheddar cheese, you know, different styles of cheese. And then it's the way I make the dough, too. I roll it up. I get the flour and all of the ingredients that you need to make the dough. I make the bottom of the pizza from scratch. But you can just buy a dough and fill it to the brim also—especially if you got the whole hood waiting on a slice. Either way you're official like a referee with a whistle. One thing about my recipe is it got that flavor. So when you bite into it you're tasting multiple variations of good shit that you ain't really used to.

MAKES 4 SINGLE-SERVING PIZZAS

INGREDIENTS
- ¼ cup [60 ml] extra-virgin olive oil, plus more for brushing the skillet
- 2 garlic cloves, minced
- 1 tsp red pepper flakes
- 1 lb [455 g] store-bought ready-to-bake pizza dough, allowed to sit at room temperature for at least 20 minutes
- 1 15-oz [430-g] can crushed tomatoes
- 1 8-oz [230-g] ball mozzarella (shrink-wrapped; not packed in brine), torn into small pieces, or 2 cups [160 g] shredded mozzarella cheese or sharp Cheddar cheese
- 4 oz [115 g] sliced pepperoni (optional)
- 4 oz [115 g] cooked sausage (optional)
- ¼ cup [8 g] ground or finely grated Parmesan cheese

1. In a small skillet over medium-low heat, combine the olive oil, garlic, and red pepper flakes. Cook until sizzling and fragrant, about 3 minutes. Remove from the heat and set aside.

2. Preheat the broiler to high, with a rack directly beneath the heat source.

3. Divide the pizza dough into four pieces. Place a 10-in [25-cm] cast iron skillet over medium-high heat and let heat for a few minutes. Meanwhile, use your hands to press and stretch the first portion of dough into a circle about 9 in [23 cm] in diameter.

4. Lightly brush the skillet with olive oil. Carefully and evenly lay the dough circle in it. Cook for 90 seconds to 2 minutes, lifting the edge of the crust with a spatula to check that the bottom is blistered and slightly crisp. Flip the dough and, working quickly, spoon about ⅓ cup [80 ml] of crushed tomatoes over the pizza crust. Top with one-fourth of the mozzarella or Cheddar cheese and about 10 pepperoni slices or ¼ cup [28 g] cooked sausage. After 2 to 3 minutes more, the bottom should be blistered and slightly crisp and the cheese beginning to melt.

5. Remove the skillet from the heat. Scatter 1 Tbsp of Parmesan cheese over the top. Place the skillet under the broiler for about 2 minutes, until the pizza is sizzling and browned. Transfer to a plate and serve immediately, drizzling with the seasoned garlic oil at the table. Repeat with the remaining portions of the dough and toppings.

Game Night: All About the Dominoes

FEW GAMES ARE AS popular in the hood as a good game of dominoes. Yeah, it ain't a fancy, intellectual game like chess but you can best believe me and the homies can get real competitive over that shit! Hood games require hood grub. These simple favorites provide solid pick-me-ups when the homies are slamming down those tiles on the kitchen table or in the backyard. During a sunny L.A. afternoon lasting into the night, ain't nothin' better.

Eastside Cheese Quesadillas [176]

DOGGs in a Blanket [177]

Get Tha Chip Fried Chicken Wings [80]

OG Gin and Juice [133]

BEATS and BITES

Dominoes with the homies is all about kickin' back with a drink in your hand. We gotta set the mood off with the soundtrack, and my man Ill Will gave us the perfect carefree anthem with "SUMMERTIME." We keep the vibe mellow with some more throwback jams like my man Warren's "THIS DJ" and my big homie Dr. Dre's "LET ME RIDE." We keep it current with a little Calvin Harris, which still has that Cali swagger to it. Everyone's gonna be able to bounce, rock, and skate to these tracks.

~ 1 ~
SUMMERTIME
WILL SMITH

~ 2 ~
THIS DJ
WARREN G

~ 3 ~
THIS IS HOW WE DO IT
MONTELL JORDAN

~ 4 ~
LET ME RIDE
DR. DRE

~ 5 ~
SEPTEMBER
EARTH, WIND & FIRE

~ 6 ~
SO FRESH, SO CLEAN
OUTKAST

~ 7 ~
WHERE THE PARTY AT
JAGGED EDGE

~ 8 ~
SLIDE
CALVIN HARRIS

~ 9 ~
LOVE AND HAPPINESS
AL GREEN

~ 10 ~
NO DIGGITY
BLACKSTREET

Eastside Cheese Quesadillas

I gotta hand it to my Mexican homies—they know how to use that cheese the right way. You ain't really need too much to create the perfect quesadilla—just a couple tortillas and a whole heap of cheese. Cook it up 'til that cheese is all nice and melted, and boom—it's a certified snack, Jack!

SERVES 8

FOR THE CHIPOTLE SAUCE:

3   Tbsp sour cream
3   Tbsp mayonnaise
4   Tbsp [60 ml] Sriracha

FOR THE QUESADILLAS:

8   flour tortillas
2   cups [160 g] shredded Cheddar cheese
1   cup [80 g] shredded Monterey Jack cheese
6   Tbsp [85 g] unsalted butter

FOR THE FINISHING TOUCH:

2   avocados, sliced
3   Tbsp chopped fresh cilantro
2   limes, quartered

TO MAKE THE CHIPOTLE SAUCE:

In a small bowl, stir together the sour cream, mayonnaise, and Sriracha until combined. Refrigerate until ready to use.

TO MAKE THE QUESADILLAS:

1. Place the tortillas on a clean work surface and top evenly with the cheeses. Fold each tortilla in half over the cheese.

2. In a large skillet over medium heat, melt 2 Tbsp of butter. Swirl the pan to cover the bottom completely.

3. When the skillet is hot and the foam has subsided, add 2 tortillas. Cook for 2 to 3 minutes per side until golden and lightly crisp. The cheese should be gooey and melted. Carefully remove the quesadillas from the skillet and set aside, tented with aluminum foil to keep warm. Repeat with the remaining butter and quesadillas.

4. Serve immediately with the chipotle sauce and avocados on the side. Garnish everything with cilantro and limes.

DOGGs in a Blanket

PIGS in a blanket? Nah, I don't really mess with the pigs like that. My dogs in a blanket are a different story. The Top Dogg has just the recipe to put those hot dogs to use. Forget throwin' 'em on the grill—these weenies never tasted better than they do when they're rolled up. And after you're done chowing down, you might need to roll up something else...

SERVES 8

INGREDIENTS

8   hot dogs, split down the middle
2   cups [160 g] shredded sharp Cheddar cheese
1   8-oz [230 g] can crescent rolls
1   jalepeño pepper, seeded and thinly sliced
    Yellow mustard, for serving

1. Preheat the oven to 375°F [190°C], with a rack in the middle position. Line a baking sheet with aluminum foil and set aside.

2. Tightly pack each split dog with Cheddar cheese. Set aside.

3. On a clean work surface, unroll the dough and cut it into 8 triangles.

4. Lay the jalepeño slices on the dough triangles, stopping about 1 in [2.5 cm] from the points.

5. Lay 1 dog along the widest edge of a triangle. Gently roll the dough around the dog, rolling it toward the point. Place the dog in the blanket on the prepared baking sheet. Repeat with the remaining hot dogs and dough triangles.

6. Place the baking sheet in the oven and bake for 13 to 15 minutes, rotating the sheet halfway through the baking time to ensure even cooking, or until golden brown. Serve immediately with the mustard, if not sooner!

From Tha Beach: Seafood Remix

I'M NOT BIG ON HANDLING SEAFOOD, but I sure love eating it. You might remember seeing me on TV with my homegirl Martha, when they tried to have me grab some real live lobster straight outta the tank. I wasn't trying to hold those lobsters as they wriggled around, and I damn sure ain't about to try and pick up no crab! I've seen the claws on those suckers, man—they're not about to slice one of my paws off! Sprinkled with spices, doused with juices, and cooked up with some butter though? Ooh-wee! A seafood platter always sets the party off, so see about these recipes and prepare to be the big fish at your next get together. Ya dig?

Down Under
Lobster Thermidor [74]
The Deadliest
Crab Legs [182]   Bossin'
Up Shrimp
Cocktail [183]   California
Rollin' [184]   French
Connect 75 [144]

BEATS and BITES

C'mon man...you see the theme here. "CALIFORNIA ROLL" ain't just one of my classic records, it's the namesake of the bomb-est roll on the menu. My guys Timbo and Jigga told you how to dine like a boss with that "LOBSTER AND SCRIMP," while my guys Migos be whippin' it up like it's "STIR FRY." You gettin' hungry yet? Yeah, the aquatic theme is strong, but I don't know about eating no "JELLYFISH." I had to slide that Ghostface jam on here though—certified classic.

~1~
CALIFORNIA ROLL
SNOOP DOGG, FEATURING PHARRELL WILLIAMS
AND STEVIE WONDER

~2~
STIR FRY
MIGOS

~3~
KUNG FU FIGHTING
CARL DOUGLAS

~4~
(SITTIN' ON) THE DOCK OF THE BAY
OTIS REDDING

~5~
PAID IN FULL
ERIC B AND RAKIM

~6~
LOBSTER AND SCRIMP
TIMBALAND, FEATURING JAY-Z

~7~
WE GON' MAKE IT
JADAKISS, FEATURING STYLES P

~8~
LIVIN' ON A PRAYER
BON JOVI

~9~
I'M ON A BOAT
LONELY ISLAND, FEATURING T-PAIN

~10~
JELLYFISH
GHOSTFACE KILLAH, FEATURING
CAPPADONNA, SHAWN WIGS, AND TRIFE

The Deadliest Crab Legs

This was inspired by the show *The Deadliest Catch*. They go out in the ocean and collect a bunch of crabs to make money, and take a chance on losing their life. And they in Alaska so they get the best crabs you could ever find. Those are my guys. I hung out with them a couple of times—on dry land though.

But unlike those guys, I don't mess with the crab when he alive, I don't do none of that shit. I just have somebody do that process for me. You ain't gotta be a big baller to have someone take care of that either—just ask the homie behind the supermarket counter. Rather them than me!

SERVES 4

INGREDIENTS

5   Tbsp [70 g] unsalted butter
2   lb [910 g] king or snow crab legs, thawed if frozen
3   lemons, halved
1   Tbsp chopped flat-leaf parsley leaves

1. Preheat the broiler, with a rack positioned 5 in [12 cm] from the broiler unit. Line a baking sheet with aluminum foil and set aside.

2. Place 1 Tbsp of butter in a small microwave-safe dish and melt it in the microwave.

3. Place the crab legs on the prepared baking sheet and brush them with the melted butter. Put the baking sheet under the broiler for 3 to 4 minutes. Turn the crab legs and broil for 3 to 4 minutes more.

4. While the crab broils, prepare the clarified butter. In a small saucepan over low heat, melt the remaining 4 Tbsp [55 g] of butter. Pour the melted butter through a coffee filter, or cheese-cloth-lined strainer to remove the milk solids.

5. Serve the crab with the clarified butter on the side for dipping and the lemon halves for squeezing; garnish with the parsley.

Bossin' Up Shrimp Cocktail

I love any kind of seafood, especially some real good shrimp. I remember getting the late-night munchies when I was in New York City, and my nephew Dave East took me through the after-hours spot to get some of the best shrimp I ever tasted! It would go real good in this shrimp cocktail recipe, which will set your next dinner party off right.

SERVES 4

FOR THE COCKTAIL SAUCE:

1   cup [275 g] chili sauce
¼   cup [65 g] prepared horseradish
1   tsp freshly squeezed lemon juice
½   tsp cracked black pepper
½   tsp hot sauce

FOR THE SHRIMP:

¼   cup [60 ml] dry white wine
2   lemons, 1 halved, 1 sliced
1   tsp peppercorns
1   tsp salt
2   sprigs flat-leaf parsley
1   bay leaf
1   lb [455 g] shrimp, thawed if frozen

TO MAKE THE COCKTAIL SAUCE:

In a small bowl, whisk the chili sauce, horseradish, lemon juice, pepper, and hot sauce. Cover and refrigerate until ready to serve.

TO MAKE THE SHRIMP:

1. In a Dutch oven over high heat, combine 4 cups [960 ml] of water, the wine, lemon halves, peppercorns, salt, parsley, and bay leaf. Bring to a boil. Lower the heat to a simmer and cook for 10 minutes.

2. Drop the shrimp into the water and turn off the heat. Cover the pot and let sit for 3 minutes, stirring occasionally. Drain, discard the whole spices, and let the shrimp cool.

3. Peel and devein the shrimp. Refrigerate until chilled and ready to serve with the cocktail sauce and lemon slices.

California Rollin'

I met the famed sushi chef, Morimoto, at a food festival in Napa Valley a few years back. Up until that point, I never even had sushi. The homie basically showed me how to make it right there on the spiz-ot. He gave me some ingredients and I came straight to the crib home and just kept practicing. I made some for my homies and they thought it from a real spot. I don't eat raw sushi, noooo way, nu-uh. I stick with the California roll, ya dig?

Ya see with sushi, it's gotta be laid out. Rolled, measured precisely, cut, served so it looks good. It's like art. I already know what you're thinking so take this tip: Rolling blunts and rolling sushi are indeed similar. But you need more palm action to roll sushi as opposed to finger action to roll blunts. And that's one to grow on.

SERVES 8

INGREDIENTS

8   nori sheets, halved crosswise
4   cups [720 g] cooked white rice, preferably sushi rice
½ cup [70 g] sesame seeds, toasted
2   avocados, julienned
1   cucumber, julienned
½ pineapple, julienned
2   cups [135 g] shredded crabmeat
Soy sauce, for serving
Wasabi, for serving
Sliced peeled fresh ginger, for serving

1. Line a bamboo sushi mat with plastic wrap. Place one nori sheet, shiny-side down, on the mat.

2. Evenly spread ¼ cup [45 g] of cooked rice over the nori sheet. Lightly wet your hands and firmly press down on the rice to compress it. Sprinkle 1½ tsp of sesame seeds over the rice, pressing them lightly to adhere.

3. Carefully turn the nori over onto a clean work surface, rice-side down. The filling will be placed on the nori, not the rice.

4. Working with one ingredient at a time, place one-eighth of the avocado in a thin line across the bottom edge (closest to you) of the nori. Place the cucumber next to it, followed by the pineapple and crabmeat, being careful not to overfill the roll.

5. Holding the filling in place with your fingers, place your thumbs under the rice layer and tightly roll the sushi away from you, tucking in the edges tightly and removing the plastic wrap as you roll. Cut the roll crosswise into 6 to 8 pieces and set aside on a large plate. Repeat with the remaining nori and filling ingredients.

6. Serve with soy sauce, wasabi, and fresh ginger.

THA FLIP

Believe it or not there was a time when I couldn't roll one up, too. Put half a piece of nori, shiny-side down on a clean surface. Spread 3 Tbsp of cooked rice to cover one-third of the nori sheet. Top with your fillings and roll into a cone. Seal the edges with a little water and you've got yourself a hand roll—just as tasty. Yeah, just like that.

ACKNOWLEDGMENTS

Firstly, I would like to thank God for blessing me with my wife and kids.

Secondly, shout out to the publishing and creative teams who helped put my vision together for *From Crook to Cook*: Chronicle Books, Snoopadelic Books, and MERRY JANE.

Finally, a special message to all my family members, homies who have lived or traveled with me, and, of course, my homegirl Martha Stewart...thank you all for the gift of sharing recipes over the years, cooking for friends around the world, and celebrating the joy and meaning of a good meal together!

Biography

Snoop Dogg is an entertainment icon who has reigned for more than two decades as an unparalleled force. He has raised the bar as an entertainer, paving the way for many artists and is recognized as a global innovator. Snoop Dogg is at the forefront of popular culture with his award-winning music, film and TV roles—both in front and behind the camera—as well as his entrepreneurial ventures and philanthropic efforts. Snoop Dogg defines entertainment and hip-hop history.

Snoop Dogg was born and raised in Long Beach, California. His mother gave him the nickname Snoop because she thought he looked like one of the characters in the Peanuts cartoon. After graduating from high school, Snoop started making music along with his cousin, Nate Dogg, and friend, Warren G, and then began working with the legendary Dr. Dre. Throughout his music career, Snoop has set records with #1 albums and songs on the Billboard charts, including: His debut album, *Doggystyle* and songs "Gin & Juice," "Who Am I? (What's My Name?)," "Nuthin' But A 'G' Thang," "Next Episode," "Beautiful," "Drop It Like It's Hot," "Signs," "Sensual Seduction," "I Wanna Rock," and "Young, Wild and Free." Released in 2018, Snoop Dogg's Gospel album, *Bible Of Love*, stayed #1 on the Billboard charts for seven weeks.

With deep roots in the community, Snoop can be found spending his time coaching kids in The Snoop Youth Football League, a non-profit organization he founded in 2005 to provide the opportunity for inner-city children to participate in youth football, and supporting various global charities.

Known for his smooth and charismatic personality, Snoop Dogg is also an Emmy-nominated host of VH1's *Martha & Snoop Potluck Dinner* and the host of TBS's *Snoop Dogg Presents The Joker's Wild*. Snoop positioned himself as a savvy and forward-thinking leader in the cannabis space. In late 2015, Snoop founded MERRY JANE, a media platform which sits at the crossroads of pop culture, business, politics, health, and the new generation of normalized, sophisticated cannabis culture for all. He also launched his very own cannabis product line of edibles and flowers, "Leafs by Snoop." With a passion that spans categories, Snoop truly is one of the most versatile artists the world has ever seen.

Snoop Dogg has been married to his high school sweetheart, Shante Broadus, for more than 20 years. They have three beautiful children: sons Corde Broadus and Cordell Broadus, and daughter Cori Broadus. Their family resides in Los Angeles, California.

Index

MIX
Paper from responsible sources
FSC
www.fsc.org
FSC™ C136333

EDITOR
Camaren Subhiyah
DESIGN BY
Sebit Min and Andrew Teoh

10 9 8 7

EDITOR FOR MERRY JANE
Noah Rubin
ADDITIONAL WRITING
Conan Milne

MERRY JANE